Local action on alcohol problems

Edited by

David Robinson, Philip Tether, and John Teller

Tavistock/Routledge

First published 1989
by Routledge
11 New Fetter Lane, London EC4P 4EE

Typeset by Laserscript Ltd, Mitcham, Surrey
Printed and bound in Great Britain by
MacKays of Chatham PLC, Chatham, Kent

British Library Cataloguing in Publication Data

Robinson, David, *1941–*
Local action on alcohol problems.
1. Great Britain. Alcoholism. Prevention
I. Title II. Teller, John III. Tether, Philip
362.2'9286

ISBN 0-415-00986-3

Local action on alcohol problems

Contents

Contributors

Peter M. Abel Director, Hillingdon Action Group on Alcohol Misuse, Uxbridge, Middlesex (formerly Social Worker, County of Avon).

David Arnold National Drinkwise Day Campaign Co-ordinator, Health Education Authority, London (formerly Health Promotion Officer, Bristol and Weston Health Authority and District Co-ordinator, South West 'Understanding Alcohol' programme).

John G. Bligh General Practitioner, Chester.

S.C. Brooks Consultant, Accident and Emergency, Kent and Canterbury Hospital, Canterbury.

Robin Bunton Co-ordinator, Alcohol Concern Wales/Gweithgor Alcohol Cymru, Cardiff (formerly Education Officer, Avon Council on Alcoholism).

John Cook Senior Probation Officer, Eastleigh.

Richard Cyster Director, Gloucestershire Council on Alcohol, Cheltenham (formerly Alcohol Project Officer, Department of Community Medicine, King's College School of Medicine and Dentistry).

Audrey Harvey Director, Alcohol Advisory and Counselling Service, Aberdeen.

George Hepburn Director, Tyne and Wear Foundation, Newcastle upon Tyne (formerly Director, Greater London Alcohol Advisory Service).

John Knight Co-founder of the Campaign Against Drinking and Driving, Cambridge.

Mike McKnight Principal Engineer Road Safety, Road Safety Unit, City Engineers Department, Birmingham City Council, Birmingham.

Deirdre McLean Women's Services Development Officer, Alcohol Recovery Project, London (formerly Community Alcohol Problems Prevention Officer, Community Alcohol Team, Narborough, Leicester).

Bernard Miller Sheffield Magistrates Court, Sheffield (formerly Chairman, Sheffield Licensing Committee).

Ken Painter District Health Education Officer, Southmead Health Education Department, Southmead Hospital, Westbury-on-Trym, Bristol.

Rhona Panton Principal Pharmacist, Education and Training, West Midlands Regional Health Authority, Birmingham.

Richard G. Quail Divisional Welfare Manager and Co-ordinator, Alcohol Education Unit, London Regional Transport, London.

Peter Rørstad Director, North-East Council on Addictions, Newcastle upon Tyne (formerly Director, North-East Council on Alcoholism).

Derek Sangster (formerly Honorary Secretary, Parrot and Palm Development Agency).

Peter Steel Manager, Client Services, Avon Council on Alcoholism, Bristol.

John A. Stevenson Chief Inspector, Operations Support Division, Humberside Police, Hull (formerly Sub-Divisional Inspector, Hull Central Sub-Division, Humberside Police).

David Taylor Senior Probation Officer, Humberside Probation Service, Hull.

John Teller Director, Avon Council on Alcoholism.

Peter Tomson General Practitioner, Abbots Langley.

Jeanne Wesson Drink-Drive Project Leader, Aquarius, Birmingham (formerly Drink-Drive Education Officer, Aquarius Court Alcohol Service).

Richard Whittington H.M. Coroner for Districts of Birmingham and Solihull, Birmingham.

Roy Youdale Trade Union Studies Tutor, Avon Centre for Trade Union Studies, Filton, Bristol.

Preventing alcohol problems: an introduction to the case studies

Introduction

> To control growth in alcohol misuse and in the harm it causes requires preventive action in which central government, local government, the health professions and institutions, the business sector and trade unions, voluntary bodies, and the people of the United Kingdom as individuals can all recognize and play their separate parts.
>
> (*Drinking Sensibly*, DHSS, 1981: 65)

This volume of case studies has been produced as a direct result of the interest shown in *Preventing Alcohol Problems: A Guide to Local Action* (Tether and Robinson, 1986). That guide was intended, in part, to stimulate further action at the local level. But in the main it drew together information on the many innovative and interesting developments already taking place. The underlying theme of the guide was 'if it can be done in one locality it can be done in every locality'.

These case studies describe some existing local prevention work. They are presented here not so much as examples of 'new directions', but for the rather more pragmatic reason of explaining why the activity was established, how it developed, who was involved, what went well, what went wrong, and what would be done differently in the light of experience. For experience needs to be shared. And these case studies are designed to do just that, so that those who consider that some activity is worthwhile or interesting will not need to completely re-invent the wheel.

The structure of this volume is very similar to *Preventing Alcohol Problems: A Guide to Local Action.* That is because the ideas which were suggested to us came in part from the request we made at the end of each chapter for additional information, updating, examples of good practice, and anything else which might usefully be given a wider circulation.

Alcohol consumption, prevention, and policy

Since 1950 there has been an increase of approximately 50 per cent in world-wide alcohol consumption. The three main features of this period have been that:

the largest increases have been in the previously lowest consumption countries;

there has been a decrease in the difference between countries' general drinking patterns – so that in predominantly beer-drinking countries there has been rapid increase in wine and spirit consumption, while in predominantly wine-drinking countries the biggest increase has been in spirits and beer; and

within countries, the biggest increase has been in those sections of the population which were previously the lowest consumers – women and young people.

These processes within the world-wide alcohol market have been mirrored in the UK where, since 1950, overall alcohol consumption has doubled; accounted for by a 60 per cent increase in beer consumption, a 350 per cent increase in spirits, and a 600 per cent increase in the consumption of wine.

The well recognized benefits of drinking alcohol in moderate amounts are that it stimulates the digestive juices, loosens the tongue a little, and encourages a sense of general well-being. These are all significant benefits, particularly in today's world with its fast and often indigestible foods, its demands on us to be socially competent in an ever-widening range of situations and fleeting relationships, and its stresses and strains which increase our need to be able to relax. So we should not be surprised that the majority of people in most countries like to have a drink, whether it is a glass of beer, or wine, or distilled spirit.

If everyone drank moderately then alcohol would cease to be one of the chief causes of contemporary health and social problems. Clearly, not everyone does drink moderately. In fact, alcohol consumption above a moderate level has been found to be a significant contributory factor in almost every situation in which harm is done by people to themselves or to others, whether this is in relation to physical and mental health, family and social relationships, work, or the law.

Given the ubiquity of alcohol and the contribution of alcohol to so many contemporary health and social problems it has become widely recognized that there is no such thing as 'the' alcohol problem. There are many alcohol problems and there are many problems in which alcohol consumption is a component. This collection of case studies is based on the assumption that in every major area of contemporary life there are people getting into difficulties to a greater or lesser extent because of their drinking. It follows from this that there is in every area of contemporary life a potential for prevention. The case studies reported here show how, in some localities, this potential has been turned into action.

The UK case studies are consistent with the broader world-wide concern with the prevention of alcohol problems and the promotion of health. The International Conference of Primary Health Care, organized by WHO and UNICEF, reaffirmed in its Declaration of Alma Ata (1978) that health is a fundamental human right. It stressed that the attainment of the highest possible level of health requires the action of many other social and economic sectors in addition to the health sector and then, echoing the Thirtieth World Health Assembly, 1977, set as a target for governments, international organizations, and the whole world community: 'the attainment by all the peoples of the world by the year 2000 of a level of health that will permit them to lead a socially and economically productive life.'

The Declaration of Alma Ata (Section V) emphasizes that 'governments have a responsibility for the health of their people'. But just as governments must provide 'adequate health and social measures' so the people of any country have the 'right and duty to participate individually and collectively in the planning and implementation of their health care' (Section IV). As part of the development of the policy climate to make more likely both the government action and the public participation, the Ottawa Charter was presented and adopted in 1986 at the First International Conference on Health Promotion. The Charter recognized the increasing attention being given to the 'new public health' and re-emphasized the key thrust of the Declaration of Alma Ata by stressing the need for health promotion to put health 'on the agenda of all policy makers *in all sectors and at all levels*'. It is within this broad policy climate that current debate about how to combat alcohol problems is taking place.

National drug and alcohol policies are increasingly being developed in the form of overall strategic objectives with, in some cases, action plans to achieve these objectives and, in just a few cases, indicators of how to evaluate those actions. For example in the draft National Health Policy on Alcohol in Australia presented to the Ministerial Council on Drug Strategy, in 1986, objectives were set in relation to availability, price and taxation, advertising and marketing, and other legal controls, together with policies in relation to education, treatment, the non-governmental sector, and research. Strategies for achieving those objectives were set out together with evaluation indices. The indices on advertising, for example, were:

- the restriction of direct advertising of alcohol on television to those periods scheduled for adult viewing;
- the reduction of the tax deductibility of expenditure on alcohol advertising to 0 per cent;

- the elimination of direct advertising of alcoholic beverages, as distinct from corporate identification of sponsorship, in conjunction with sporting and cultural activities;
- evidence of reduced lifestyle advertising;
- evidence of reduced targeting of specific groups in the advertising of alcohol.

The good sense of such objectives, strategies for action, and indices for judging progress is undeniable. But the trick, of course, is to turn them from policy statements into policy practice. Some of those who call for national control policies do not appear to appreciate the range and complexity of already existing policies and activities. In fact they sometimes seem to be suggesting that there is no national policy at all. But, of course, every country in which there is alcohol has a *de facto* national policy. We may or may not like that policy, but that is a separate matter.

A detailed map of the current policy terrain in any country would reveal a wide range of statutory, commercial, voluntary, professional, service sector and other agencies, groups, and organizations involved in some way with alcohol and related problems. At government level alone, for example, there will be many ministries or departments of state that play some role in relation to some aspect of alcohol regulation, taxation and legislation, importation and exportation, production and distribution, promotion and sale, or the consequences of consumption. The laws, regulations, and activities of these governmental and many other organizations constitute the country's national alcohol policy.

Much debate about how best to combat alcohol problems is rather over simple in two major respects: in relation to issues and in relation to organizations. The issues, for instance, are often no more firmly delineated than in calls for 'something to be done' about some high profile problems and target groups such as: young people, advertising, drinking and driving, taxes, customs controls, pregnant women, and so on. All of these are important issues. But since the list could be extended endlessly it helps if they are grouped for purposes of both policy statement and policy practice. When matters are more systematically considered it is usually found that most discussions of alcohol issues tend to be primarily concerned with either:

employment and the market,
education,
advertising and the media,
health and safety, or
law and order.

Within these constellations of issues there are, of course, limitless specifics. Within 'law and order' there are, for example, matters to do with:

illicit production,
illegal sale or purchase,
importation, trade, or tax offences,
public drunkenness,
liquor licensing, and
drinking and driving.

Yet even this is too simple a level for mapping the real terrain of alcohol policy issues. Within the 'drinking and driving' issue, for example, there is a multitude of policy strands such as:

motorists' rights,
apprehension procedures,
adequacy of breath test apparatus,
police records,
court practice, and
sentencing policy

together with related concerns such as:

highway construction,
surface markings and lighting,
car design,
learner driver education, and
general public safety education.

In any policy constellation of related policy issues, then, there are many levels of policy which go to make up the real policy terrain. All this is obvious. But does it matter? In particular, does it matter for those concerned with prevention? In order to answer that question we need to consider the second major area of common over-simplification in the alcohol policy debate: organizations.

As with issues, much discussion of policy organizations is restricted to dominant groupings; often little more than:

- the government
- the helping professions
- the trade
- the law
- the general public.

All these are, of course, important. But in policy debate it is unhelpful if they are not disaggregated. There is no such thing as *a* trade or *a* professional view on alcohol. Similarly no 'government' is an entity in relation to alcohol any more than it is in relation to anything else. Governments each have many policies in relation to alcohol, each of which will be more or less explicit and more or less compatible with other policies. The recent analysis of *Alcohol Policies: Responsibilities and Relationships in British Government* (Tether and Harrison, 1988) mapped out the national policy complexity.

Local policy

The complexity of the policy terrain means that local alcohol policy cannot possibly be cultivated by every policy organization being involved in every prevention issue. The real world of alcohol consumption, policy, and prevention, therefore, is made up of policy 'networks' where the issues and the organizations meet.

Those who participate in any particular local network may not all share the same view about the nature of any particular alcohol problem or share the same view about who does or should do what, when, where, and with whom to prevent it. For policy networks are not made up of organizations and groups which agree with each other. They are made up of those who need or choose or are required to be involved in some overlapping policy area of interest and concern.

In any locality, as in any country, there will be a wide range of policy networks. There may be dominant clusters of networks concerned with policy action in relation to alcohol which may well correspond with the major constellations of policy issues mentioned earlier, such as employment and the market, education, advertising and the media, health and safety, and law and order.

While sets of dominant issues may be readily identifiable clear boundaries cannot be drawn around the policy networks. Moreover, there will be sub-networks where specific issues are focused on and fought over. And, of course, network will interact with network because policy organizations may well be involved in more than one policy network. This also means that policy cultivation in one network may drag an organization or part of an organization in one direction which may conflict with the way it is being dragged in another network. At the national level this happens most obviously with the premier policy organization, national government, where, for example, an agriculture or trade ministry may be encouraging the further development of the whisky industry while the health, law, and transport ministries may be attempting to cope with the consequences of increased consumption.

This placing of alcohol debate within the everyday business of social and political activity is essential if any realistic progress is to be made towards the cultivation of better policies to control alcohol problems. And within the real policy world – as opposed to the world of apolitical exhortation – things do change. And so they can change in the 'right' direction; as defined by those who wish to control alcohol problems. Three current changes are particularly important.

First is the change in policy climate which was mentioned earlier. And here the movements for health for all by the year 2000 and for healthy public policy, including the healthy cities concept, are playing their part in trying to raise the issue of health higher up the political agenda in many localities. The aim is to make health less an unintended consequence of other policy action and less a residual category or second order concern and more a defining characteristic of public policy.

The second way in which things can change for the better is by the very nature of most social policy cultivation. Rather than pressing for *a* coherent policy – under which all action is geared to securing some well-defined objective – the reality of the policy terrain demands that a desired policy-in-action, rather than merely policy-on-paper, can only be cultivated through a process of 'partisan mutual adjustment' (Lindblom, 1965). As it has recently been succinctly described:

> Agencies are 'partisan' in that they pursue their own interests but they are capable of 'mutual adjustment', in that they adapt to the decisions made by other agencies, or attempt to influence them through negotiation, bargaining, and manipulation. The policy which emerges may not be the theoretical optimum, but it will be one over which agreement has been reached, and which therefore stands some chance of being implemented. In Lindblom's analysis, 'partisan mutual adjustment' is both descriptive and prescriptive in that it purports not only to describe what happens but to recommend it as a 'democratic' way of making policy.
>
> (Tether and Harrison, 1988)

The task then for those who want to push local alcohol policy in the 'right' direction is to get involved in the policy cultivation process. This is clearly possible in the complexity of organizations which make up the policy terrain. It is important to do so when the policy climate, as now, is conducive to change.

The third positive sign for change is that there has been a growing emphasis on things other than *national* policy in relation to alcohol. Let us be quite clear; national prevention policies are certainly essential. But concentration on action at the national level to the exclusion of any serious consideration of anything else is mistaken. It implies, unhelpfully, that the only worthwhile response to contemporary health and social problems is global action by central government. Such a viewpoint diverts attention from the wealth or other – sectoral and local – prevention resources which are so often unrecognized and, therefore, untapped.

No local prevention policy package will, of course, be able to change such things as customs regulations, retailing law, the drink-driving law, or the Chancellor of the Exchequer's taxation policies. Nevertheless, many effective and sensible measures can be taken at the local level without the backing of legislation, massive funding, or central government commitments. What is required locally is the careful identification and cataloguing of resources, together with specific intervention by interested people, at the right time, through appropriate organizations which will encourage, promote, and co-ordinate minor, but important, changes in existing practices and procedures.

The exploration of local resources and the systematic exploration of the opportunities they provide to prevent alcohol problems do not reduce the need for an integrated and consistent national policy. However, those concerned about alcohol problems in particular localities should not wait for national initiatives. They should create policy at the periphery where the problems and so many of the resources are located and where, moreover, developments serve as models for national policy-makers. For good practice at the local level today is often, as any political analyst knows, tomorrow's central policy.

The development of a local strategy and its spread would be encouraged if the locality has a group which is clearly seen to be responsible for disseminating knowledge about the prevention of alcohol problems, which lobbies local organizations to develop their prevention potential, and which is the repository of ideas about good practice and a clearing house for materials and knowledge of prevention developments.

Whether this focus of local prevention activity is an existing local council on alcoholism, a joint care planning team, an associated liaison committee, an alcohol forum, or an *ad hoc* local alcohol group set up specifically for the purpose, it will need to know not only about the prevention contribution which all organizations and groups of workers can make but also about the structure of these organizations, how to gain access, and who to approach.

It may be that the local action group will not just stimulate and encourage but may take responsibility itself for various local prevention activities. There may be the need to organize multi-disciplinary alcohol education, multi-professional in-service training, a public education campaign, or a range of lobbying activities in relation to national organizations which it would be inappropriate or inconvenient for any other local organization to undertake.

Similarly, it may be that the local action group is the only organization which can, with help from a local university or other institution, draw together and disseminate basic information which could be used for assessing the extent of alcohol problems in the locality or for monitoring the impact of prevention activities. Yet again, the local action group may develop teaching skills, become a repository for alcohol education materials, and even undertake prevention 'consultancies' with local organizations. In some localities there may still be very few people with any interest in or experience of working in the area of alcohol problems. The formal establishment of a group to bring together the few people that there are could be a vital first step towards significant local action.

In the first case study John Teller describes the establishment of just such a group in Avon.

References

Declaration of Alma Ata (1978) *Report of the International Conference on Primary Health Care*, WHO/UNICEF, ICPHC/PRA/70 10, Geneva: WHO.

Department of Health and Social Security (1981) *Drinking Sensibly*, London: HMSO.

Harrison, L. and Tether, P. (1987) 'The Coordination of UK Policy on Alcohol and Tobacco: the significance of organisational networks', *Policy and Politics* 15, 2: 77–90.

Lindblom, C. (1965) *The Intelligence of Democracy*, New York: Free Press.

Tether, P. and Harrison, L. (1988) *Alcohol Policies: Responsibilities and Relationships in British Government*, Addiction Research Centre, Universities of Hull and York.

Tether, P. and Robinson, D. (1986) *Preventing Alcohol Problems: A Guide to Local Action*, London: Tavistock.

Putting prevention on the agenda

John Teller

After years of being told that the job of a local alcohol advisory centre is to help people with drinking problems it was not easy to switch our attention to the issue of how to prevent them. Our focus was on alcoholism and our job was to get people to come for 'help' or 'treatment'. In the late 1970s the community we served was bombarded with messages which confirmed their view that alcoholics were a special, somehow different, group of people who, at best, required the specialist techniques offered by the medical profession.

A review of what people actually asked for when they contacted our centre during 1982 revealed some interesting facts. A large number of people wanted to know the relative strengths of different alcoholic drinks. Professionals wanted to know how they could be trained to identify problem drinkers. Some others wanted to know what they could do to prevent the spread of alcohol problems in their community. It was this latter group who interested us the most because we had been scratching our heads wondering not only what 'preventing alcohol problems' meant but also where the resources would come from when we found out.

A breakthrough, of sorts, came when two of us presented to the committee of our Centre a picture of alcohol-related harm in the community as opposed to the level of alcoholism. This showed that there was, for example, a far greater risk of dying from an alcohol-related road accident than from cirrhosis of the liver. But the committee and the staff of the Centre were then split over whether or not road accidents were our business. There was also a great fear that using the Centre's resources on prevention would reduce the level of help available to alcoholics. Although we promised that this would, of course, not happen the truth is that, at the time, we did not know. We certainly failed to realize that if we marketed our service as one that promoted sensible drinking our referral rate from people with severe alcohol problems – alcoholics – would also increase sharply. On reflection, it is only commonsense that they would be more willing to approach an agency which was not concerned with 'alcoholics only'.

A structure for taking prevention seriously

But still there was a worry over the move to prevention. An uneasy compromise was reached later in 1982 when two new sub-committees were formed: Prevention and Education and Treatment and Rehabilitation. The latter followed the well-trodden path of developing counselling and residential services. The former, not surprisingly, had difficulties from the outset. It had no resources and, worst of all, no ideas other than the general feeling that prevention was important. Arguments broke out about whether the training of counsellors belonged to 'education' or 'treatment'. Were not trained counsellors preventing alcohol problems?

At the same time a group had formed in Bath to discuss alcohol under the auspices of the Avon Council on Alcoholism. This group included teachers, AA members, probation officers, Samaritans, licensed victuallers, and the police. Among their many concerns were licensing issues, advertising, and lack of counselling services. As with our own committee the Bath group, known as the Forum, was drawn like moths to the light of establishing a counselling service, which it did. Attempts to get prevention issues on to the agenda of the Forum failed. At that time, in 1982, it was difficult to assess whether this was because we still did not know what prevention was, whether we knew but were frightened of the work, or whether we, as the 'experts', wanted to hang on to our status by undermining the true involvement of others.

One person declared that we were naïve to assume that local forums of local people wanted to do anything anyway. The facts seemed to bear him out. For example, attendance of the Forums was sporadic. Getting them to concentrate on an 'issue' for 90 minutes when meetings were three months apart was difficult. People seemed to want hand-me-down answers and solutions rather than to engage in serious debate leading to the generation of innovative ideas. All this made us realize that we 'alcohologists' could not expect ideas and action to emerge from groups of people whose knowledge about alcohol was thin and who were, in their own right, very busy people.

Consequently, we applied for and received a grant to appoint an education officer who would manage a library and information service, train professionals, and be accountable to the prevention and education sub-committee. The true potential of this post was only realized late into the period of his appointment. For example, training courses for Forum members (others had started) and for professionals tended to focus on alcohol and its effects and the services available. Only later did we realize that without an alternative focus people would continue to be drawn to 'doing something' about alcoholics – and then simply refer them on. Courses now always contain sessions on: What will stop you from putting your knowledge into practice? What steps can you take to minimize this? And, who else do you need to approach to gain support for your desire to act on your knowledge? These sessions bring to the fore the fact that organizational constraints must be identified and attacked before a change in working practices is possible.

Identifying specific targets

The importance of target groups emerged in 1984 when a number of concerns and events came together. The prevention and education sub-committee had for the first time been asked to set objectives for the forthcoming year. This was an enlightening experience. The committee and staff had to prune a massive list of ideas into a workable set of objectives with identified resources. At the same time one of the Forums in south Bristol wanted to do something for young people in the area. Few young people are alcoholics. We were, therefore, talking about prevention for the first time. Then our library and information service identified a heavy demand for videos, tape-slide shows, posters, leaflets, and trigger films for a variety of groups such as young people, women, the over-60s, etc. Finally, the Avon Drinking and Driving Forum consisting of police, road-safety, and health education staff launched a local competition aimed at 16–18-year-old road users.

The combination of these four sets of activities forced us to recognize that shortage of resources at local level requires committees and forums to set objectives, prioritize, and tailor their efforts and products to the needs of specific target groups. The potential of local prevention groups can only be realized if their activities reflect members' concerns and if the target groups are involved.

But which target groups? There are young people, male young people, female black young people – road users, lorry drivers, cyclists, pedestrians, etc. We are learning that we have to become more sophisticated in terms of market research and marketing. We have to take account of local statistics before we choose between leaflet, video, local radio, or conference as the appropriate medium. We have to be clear about which facts about drinking we want to convey to which group and why. We have to listen to the concerns of local traders, parents, and magistrates and help them act on these rather than concentrate on our own concerns.

In conclusion

From being a committee that could not stay away from 'treatment' the prevention and education sub-committee is now one that has produced information which is increasingly used by counsellors seeing 'alcoholics'. The value of learning about what sensible drinking should have been for our clients if they had had the information earlier is rated highly by counsellors and clients. The tensions, however, remain. People whose primary role is treatment still fear that problem drinkers may get a poor deal if prevention work continues – in spite of a six-fold increase in resources and use of the service.

Alcohol and information

Introduction

The chapters in this section deal primarily with education and information for the general public. Other parts of this book contain case studies which deal with education for specific sectors of the population such as those people who are in accident and emergency departments or who are in specific places of employment. Running through the many and varied calls for prevention have been competing claims about what is the best preventive approach, all of which reflect differing views about what the prime focus of prevention should be. For some it is problem drinkers; for others it is drinking attitudes; for yet others it is alcohol itself. Associated with each focus is some idea of what role information and education have to play.

An information component is usually seen as central by those whose preventive approach concentrates on the problem drinkers. The primary preventive aim is to devise ways of ensuring that people are aware of and recognize the early signs of problem drinking in themselves and in others. For members of the general public this means asking themselves questions about alcohol and its effects. Alcoholics Anonymous and many treatment agencies, education groups, and branches of the media have developed checklists of varying degrees of complexity with a view to encouraging people to calculate how much they drink, to decide whether they have a particular alcohol problem, and to recognize where to go for help, advice, and support in the event of discovering a sufficient number of warning signs.

The preventive aim for those who focus on unhealthy drinking habits is, again, basically an information and education one designed to encourage a more healthy approach to the use and place of alcohol in everyday life. Such an approach is reflected in the concern for *Drinking Sensibly* (DHSS, 1981) and grows naturally out of a large body of socio-cultural field research over the past fifty years which has focused on everyday drinking habits and associated rates of alcohol problems in different national, cultural, ethnic, and religious communities.

The information component of the approach which focuses on alcohol itself is concerned primarily with raising public awareness of policy options and possibilities, and creating a climate of opinion for change. In the light of prohibition experience in the USA and other examples of drastic controls over the availability of alcohol, it is clear that a highly restrictive regime does lead to lower consumption levels and a decline in the rate of various alcohol problems. But, of course, tight control needs political clout and is only achieved in the long term with substantial public support, while the controls themselves are apt to be expensive and may be seen to outweigh the benefits. Such costs include resentment of the system by those who consider themselves to be normal drinkers, an increase in the production of illicit liquor, difficulties with law enforcement, loss of tax revenues, and the reduction in personal and social enjoyment which drinking alcohol provides for large sections of the population of most countries.

Prevention really is 'everybody's business', which means that everyone must examine their own drinking habits and attitudes. For educators and helpers this must be done before others can be taught, guided, or helped. It also means a shift from an exclusive preoccupation with the dependent drinker towards concern with the full range of alcohol-related problems which can be experienced by anyone who drinks unwisely, intemperately, or inappropriately. Some people, of course, because of who they are or what they do are considered to be particularly at risk.

Uncertainty is widespread about alcohol, its effects, how to handle it, how to recognize problems in oneself and other people, and how to respond to such problems. Thus uncertainty is due not simply to lack of knowledge. Our society has ambiguous and equivocal attitudes towards alcohol which make it difficult for us to appraise objectively our own drinking habits and those of other people.

Many people are ignorant about alcohol and the nature, range, and extent of alcohol-related problems. Unhelpful beliefs and attitudes abound, ranging from the belief that the ability to drink large amounts of alcohol is 'manly' to the conviction that alcohol is an indispensable adjunct to every festive and social occasion. Unhelpful behaviour in relation to alcohol includes drinking to excess, regular solitary drinking, drinking on inappropriate occasions, drinking to bolster confidence, and encouraging someone else to drink inappropriately. Alcohol education should aim to erode these unhelpful attitudes, promote healthier and safer ones, and, in short, encourage sensible drinking. John Teller describes how the Avon Council on Alcoholism developed its simple leaflet for young people geared to get across the 'sensible drinking' message.

One of the weaknesses of much alcohol education is that it fails to identify the attitudes and behaviour which it hopes to promote. Often, the material is entirely negative – it is clear what it is against but not what it is for. To overcome this deficiency, it would be helpful if alcohol educators in any locality could agree a set of simple and straightforward 'messages' about alcohol, to make explicit the changes they are working towards, and to provide a framework for learning.

Alcohol Concern, the national alcohol agency, produces a bi-monthly journal, *Alcohol Concern*, which is free to individuals or organizational subscribers. Alcohol Concern is also in the process of building up a collection of books and other resources which alcohol educators will be able to draw upon. Membership of Alcohol Concern will enable any individual or organization concerned about or involved with responding to alcohol-related problems to participate directly in national debate and action. The address is Alcohol Concern, 305 Gray's Inn Road, London, WC1X 8QF.

The majority of the general public will be unlikely to be in contact with any specific alcohol agency or specific educational campaign and may be untouched by many of the other prevention activities outlined in this guide. Any local prevention strategy must, therefore, include education aimed at 'the general public'. This means that all participants in the local prevention strategy should know something of the issues and techniques surrounding public health education so that, if called upon, they can play an effective part. Of course, it is open to any group or organization to undertake public education on its own and, in some cases, this may be particularly appropriate. The fire service may want to publicize the relation of alcohol to fire accidents and the local home safety committee may want to alert the general public to the links between alcohol and home accidents. But whatever the focus of public education, those who take part in it should clearly understand that there are many opportunities for public education.

In his description of Drinkwise London, George Hepburn not only describes who did what but also sets out the characteristics of the vital steering group which managed to deliver such a complicated and comprehensive range of activities and events. Hepburn emphasizes the importance of financial support for an enterprise as wide ranging as Drinkwise London '86 but stresses, very importantly, that drinkwise campaigns are only one part of a broader programme of educational and prevention activities. It is precisely because they are part of a broader programme that the necessary resources from a broad range of local agencies can be mobilized to actually deliver during the Drinkwise week. It is understandable that after such an exhausting campaign he and his colleagues might be rather pessimistic. Actually, he should not be because the general consensus has been that Drinkwise London, like similar events in other parts of the country, plays a vital role in not only raising general public awareness and consciousness but in actually forcing organizations to work together for a common purpose and this provides structures which can be mobilized for other events and activities.

In contrast with Drinkwise London the Youth Matters exhibition described by David Arnold was very much more small scale, low key, and focused. Here the emphasis was on drawing together agencies and organizations which had something to offer to young people and, as Arnold describes, even mounting such a small event is not easy. The lessons learnt from Info '86 meant that Youth Matters '87 was better organized and considered to be more relevant by people who attended. It also shows what can be done without the thousands of pounds that a Drinkwise event requires.

There are many opportunities in any locality for promoting educational messages. Although they may be less glamorous than appearing on television they can be very effective. The Manchester Regional Committee for Cancer Education, for example, used a panel of speakers over an extended period of time to give talks to a large number of small groups. This contact and re-contact with a large number of people was found to be more effective for this task than traditional mass-media approaches. In any locality there are many societies and groups which are always on the look-out for speakers. Local alcohol educators could publicize the fact that they are available to give talks and to lead discussion groups. Local political parties, for example, usually have a programme of meetings with invited speakers. Alcohol educators could make a very useful start towards influencing the local political system by talking at these events.

Although there are many educational opportunities and many ways of reaching sections of the general public, the mass media remain particularly important since they can, in their various forms, reach almost everyone. It is vital for local prevention workers to be able to use these media with knowledge, skill, and confidence.

However, the local media will not be interested in dry 'facts' or unattractive information. Material for the local press must be interesting and stimulating. Curious and unexpected facts often make the best basis for a story. Where possible the material ought to be given a 'human interest' angle.

Participants in the local prevention strategy should go out of their way to make contact, for example, with local journalists and especially, if the paper has one, with the health correspondent. Material is more likely to be used by the local press if the contributors are known and the paper understands something of the local prevention strategy, how its various components fit together, and what the various participants in it are trying to do. Similarly, it is important for participants to learn something of the journalists' requirements and what will constitute a useful and interesting story.

There are not many people who have had more experience of working with the local media in relation to alcohol issues than Peter Rørstadt and his colleagues in Newcastle. Rørstadt's chapter describes the wide range of those working relationships and emphasizes the vital necessity for seeing relationships over the long term and also seeing them as being of mutual benefit. Many local organizations feel used by the media while many others seek merely to use the media themselves. The North-East experience has shown how press, radio, and television companies will learn how to work together with local alcohol agencies so that in partnership they can provide an information and education component to local activities which neither could provide alone.

One important issue which must be dealt with concerns language and approach. A great deal of press reporting on alcohol issues – precisely because it has to be easily readable, interesting, and eye-catching – is less helpful than it might otherwise be because of the concentration on 'alcoholics' or because of a laboured jokiness. If the participants in a local prevention strategy can get the local press to emphasize the variety of alcohol-related problems and to report them seriously a great deal of progress will have been made. Ken Painter's piece on the Winabike competition illustrates, among other things, the importance of establishing good relations with the local media in relation to specific events.

The task for any local prevention group is to be an authoritative voice on prevention and alcohol matters. The aim should be for local radio, press, and television companies automatically to come to the group whenever there is a need for advice about or comment on some national or local alcohol issue. One way of developing this relationship with local media personnel is for the local council on alcoholism or other appropriate group to organize meetings, conferences, and seminars. Such events are of mutual benefit, enabling the media to explain their requirements and opportunities to participants in the local prevention strategy and allowing the prevention group to explain to the media the range of problems that exist, the range of local facilities that are available, and the range of major issues that lie behind the broad heading of 'the prevention of alcohol problems'.

Reference

Department of Health and Social Security (1981) *Drinking Sensibly*, London: HMSO.

Sensible drinking: leaflets for target groups

John Teller

Between 1981 and 1985 the Alcohol Advisory Centre in Bristol employed four people in its agency to run the alcohol library and information service. Originally conceived as a way of responding to the numerous requests for information there was a growing feeling that the team was being buffeted by the endless variety of requests it received, such as:

- 'I'm doing a school project on alcoholics. Can you help?'
- 'I'm doing economics at college. I want something on investment of brewers in advertising. Have you got anything?'
- 'I'm a doctor. A patient has just asked me whether fructose speeds up the metabolism of alcohol. What's the answer?'
- 'Have you got a leaflet I can give my 15-year-old daughter?'
- 'Is it O.K. for my elderly mother to drink and take medication?'

This range of requests was made more difficult to respond to by two other factors. The first was the recurrent short-term funding of the team which required us to change the staff every twelve months. The second was the variable quality of the information available nationally. We made up our minds that we would begin the process of acquiring a library of useful texts, videos, and pamphlets. We also decided we would attempt to copy the drinks trade in their techniques of marketing and tailoring their products to the needs of specific target groups.

At this time the rest of our agency was coming to terms with prevention, setting objectives, and targeting (see 'Putting Prevention on the Agenda'). Consequently, it was a relatively straightforward exercise to discuss and then agree on three targets to produce pamphlets for use during the year 1986 to 1987. The chosen target groups were young people, the over-60s, and road users.

Identifying the targets was easy. But it was more difficult to get the team to the point where they actually believed they could achieve the task. It was one thing to talk about designing, marketing, piloting, and market research. It was quite another to do them. We learned, for example, that one particular manufacturer of a dark-coloured brew had increased (slightly) the interest of 16–18-year-olds in their product after spending £7 million in six months! We had no money and no expertise – just a deadline. So we started with that.

We drew a straight line. One end said 'now'. The other, 'twelve months'. We hoped that by month 11 our produce (literature) should be sitting in boxes in our office ready for marketing. Gradually the line developed other lines, with dates and tasks attached to them. We had a flow chart but no idea what we were producing! We focused on each of the target groups and aired our grievances about what literature did exist: too dull, too patronizing, too humourless, too wordy, too medical, and so on.

Having allocated primary responsibility for each of the pieces of literature to an individual team member we all agreed the obvious: we must involve the consumers in the design and content. As soon as some rough ideas were ready we would have something to sell to potential donors. In the case of the young people's pamphlet the worker went out to schools and youth clubs and asked (eventually 300) young people their views about alcohol, listened to the questions they asked, and sought their advice about a guide. Ideas began to surface. They did not want to be told what was right or wrong. They wanted to be in charge. The paper was important. Plenty of pictures. Something for the person who lived with a heavy drinking parent.

Meanwhile we were writing to trusts, charities, and other organizations for money. Trips were made to see public relations officers and managing directors. We had a few nice lunches but no cheques. Then, one organization in London asked to see us and agreed to give us £2,000! This was exactly what we calculated would be required to produce 10,000 copies of what was now called *A DIY Guide to Sensible Drinking for Young People.*

We made contact with an art student who agreed, for £200, to do all our artwork, and three versions were submitted for scrutiny to more young people. Health and education professionals in the area were also consulted in the hope of gaining advice (and perhaps advance orders!). We found with the young people's guide that adult comments such as 'too flippant' and 'awful artwork' had to be courageously ignored if the youngsters liked it.

In spite of proofreading every page by at least six people there were still mistakes when the first 10,000 arrived. One awful omission resulted in overprinting by hand a sentence in every copy! We learned that an outsider must proofread the final draft before printing.

We also learned about the cost of anticipating failure. One order alone arrived for 5,000 copies. We just did not have the logistics worked out to cope with this and hundreds of other orders of very small quantities. The stamps, the envelopes, the invoicing were a nightmare. A new member of staff introduced us to printers' brokers who, for no charge, do all the work of hunting out the most competitive printer in the UK.

Finally, we learned the value of consulting the consumer. Heartwarming stories of young people first fingering then looking at the guides does much to help find the energy to keep going with other such projects.

The price of individual copies at 25p provided us with a sufficient margin to carry out a second print run of 20,000 after the first batch had gone in 4½ weeks. Eight weeks further on we are thinking of risking another print run of 20,000.

(P.S. May 1988 – 70,000 copies gone.)

Drinkwise

George Hepburn

Drinkwise 1986 took place in the week beginning 29 September. It was the third and most ambitious event of its kind organized in London by the Federation of London Alcohol Groups (FLAG). The aims of the week were:

- to promote sensible attitudes to drinking;
- to make facts about alcohol and its effects widely available;
- to advise on average safe limits and how to keep within them;
- to increase awareness of alcohol misuse as a problem for employers and health and social work professionals.

Drinkwise was launched by Professor Anthony Clare and a host of celebrities at the National Theatre. It featured a one-day conference on prevention for managers and policy-makers and television announcements on sensible drinking broadcast on successive weekends with helplines. There was publicity on underground escalators, advertisements in the press, and over sixty events throughout London – ranging from week-long exhibitions in shopping centres to public meetings, seminars, quizzes, and competitions.

An evaluation of the campaign has been produced by the Health Education Authority and is available from the Greater London Alcohol Advisory Service (GLAAS). Based mainly on interviews with individuals and organizations involved, it provides a critical account of the campaign which will assist in the planning of similar events in the future.

The campaign created widespread interest. An article in the *Guardian* the following week, for example, led to enquiries from other parts of the country and the 'Drinkwise model' was soon being talked about as 'the' way forward for alcohol prevention. The organizers themselves were much more cautious. They stressed that the situation in London could not be reproduced elsewhere. There is a concentrated population of 7 million with even more coming into the capital to work. There is also an extremely complicated labyrinth of thirty-three local authorities and thirty-one health districts divided between four regional health authorities; and no strategic authority for London since the demise of the GLC or effective Londonwide health planning for alcohol. There are, however, at least seventy agencies helping problem drinkers. These are mainly small, voluntary, and locally based with, arguably, only two to three workers explicitly designated for prevention.

The Drinkwise idea itself was not new. The term had been coined by Drinkwise Scotland in 1985 and, according to one director of a local council on alcohol, at least one region had worn itself out running an alcohol promotion bus round a major metropolitan area ten years ago. There is a danger of re-inventing the wheel – or of not learning sufficiently from others' experiences.

Organizing Drinkwise 1986

Drinkwise has been described as a 'grassroots' campaign – organized by alcohol agencies pooling their resources from shared interest rather than responding to a national campaign or initiative. But it would be wrong to over-emphasize the 'populist' nature of Drinkwise. A lot of groups took part once the bandwagon began to roll. But essentially Drinkwise was organized by a consortium of agencies whose representatives formed the central steering group.

Although some attempts were made to ensure the major organizations in London were involved, the group was largely self-selected and consisted of highly committed workers. The concept that Drinkwise was commonly owned by this group rather than by any individual agency was crucial to its success. FLAG was used as a neutral banner-head for the campaign, but the Drinkwise steering group became far more active and powerful than the FLAG itself for the period of the campaign. The Greater London Alcohol Advisory Service provided staff and resources to service the campaign with help from other agencies, but the decisions were made collectively. This arrangement enabled agencies to contribute funds to Drinkwise which they would never have given to each other and the Drinkwise steering group was vigilant to make sure that no single agency promoted itself on the back of the campaign. Exhibition material at the launch, for example, was carefully prepared to make sure that only the Drinkwise logo appeared.

The steering group met every three weeks for the nine months preceding the campaign. The twelve members were additionally expected to contribute to at least one sub-group which hammered out details about messages, media, funding, and so on. It was a talented group which broke new ground for most of the members involved. But it was not always easy to acknowledge that the group was short of experience, such as where to take a celebrity to lunch after he had appeared at the launch without charge! Among the characteristics of the steering group were that:

- It was task-focused. A count-down timetable was agreed and adhered to which crystallized thinking. The contrast with co-ordinating groups in the alcohol field, which contained similar faces, but no clear role, was extraordinary.
- It accepted compromises. There would be furious debate about the slogans but with a pressure to make decisions, 'know when to say "when"' was accepted even though no one was wildly excited about it.
- It worked with an open-ended product which changed and developed with circumstances. London Weekend Television's offer of sensible drinking announcements was a major formative influence on the campaign but it adapted to opportunities and promises of funding on a daily basis. Although it was agreed that escalator advertising was wanted, the final go-ahead was only given a fortnight before the campaign when the fund-raising target was reached.
- It looked after itself. There was a basis of good working relationships facilitated by the convenor who ensured that members felt included and valued. A group trip to another region to discuss their campaign and some social events helped in addition.
- It exhausted itself. The evaluation comments on the difficulty of interviewing steering group members who had gone on holiday or were on sick leave immediately after the campaign. The campaign was organized on top of the existing work of the agencies involved. Routine work suffered and the campaign atmosphere led to overwork by many of those taking part. A year after the campaign a number of members have moved to new jobs. However, membership of the group was a positive experience and has led to close inter-agency relationships. The forecast that alcohol agencies might work together more profitably on prevention than on treatment has been borne out.

The campaign itself

The campaign itself involved two-thirds of the agencies in London and achieved a far higher level of participation than the two similar events in previous years. Drinkwise aimed for a much more professional product using specially designed materials such as T-shirts, balloons, beer mats, and other regalia. Regular attractive mailings created an enthusiasm for Drinkwise and this was followed up by individual contact on the phone. Some of the other factors related to agency involvement were that:

- The campaign built on existing links between alcohol agencies who formed part of a Londonwide network.

- It was the third annual campaign and noticeable both that more groups joined in each time and that experienced campaigners set themselves more ambitious goals.

- It was able to support different levels of local activity. A campaign guide was issued in advance of the campaign suggesting possible activities and these varied considerably depending on the resources of the group.
One group, which has not taken part before, ran an all-day exhibition at a mainline rail terminus in the course of which the staff made immense strides in translating counselling skills into effective conversations with commuters.

- The different levels of experience of groups showed the need for staff to be trained about public education work. The standard of exhibition material varied enormously. Some health education units had professionally designed displays whilst other groups used posters taken from the office wall. Some people were much more confident and skilful than others in engaging people. Experience suggested that staff needed to be well motivated in working with the public. It is not just anybody who can give a baby a balloon or strike up a conversation with an Asian teenager.

- The Drinkwise message was sufficiently bland for all sorts of groups to take part. Projects working for abstinence contributed to events 'off-site' so as not to confuse their clients, and AA and Al-Anon members took part as the campaign was geared to the general population. Some events, such as the conference on service provision, were only loosely linked to the Drinkwise theme but still contributed to the overall effect.

What we learned

A great deal was learned about the practicalities of running a health campaign in which colleagues in health education had far more experience than those of us used to seeing clients or managing small or voluntary agencies. The lead-in period of nine months was barely adequate but at the same time much of the work could only be undertaken in the weeks immediately beforehand. The launch was only finalized when celebrities could commit themselves to personal appearances; work with the media had to take place at short notice. This required the group to adapt to the different time scales of the professions involved. Materials could, however, have been prepared further in advance and a number of agencies were concerned about delays in distribution as the campaign approached.

The administration of the campaign was chaotic – mainly because no one envisaged the problems of packing, distribution, and invoicing materials all over London. Extra staff were taken on and a transit van hired. By raising expectations from customers and charging for materials, Drinkwise had to deliver professionally. A large roll of corrugated paper now tucked behind an office door is a constant reminder of the reality, and it is a wonder how the service to clients continued as well as it did.

There is also much more sympathy now for the way pop groups employ 'roadies'. Setting up exhibitions for the launch of the conference involved a great deal of physical work. Early morning starts are good for *esprit de corps* but can detract from the composure required to make a speech or chair a conference. One member of the group became so confused about his role that he wore a Drinkwise T-shirt under his best suit.

Such experiences point to the need, also found in the Scottish campaign, to allow resources for administration, transport, and ancillary support. Drinkwise even invested in radio-pagers to keep key people in touch with the press officer, but no amount of such ingenuity could overcome the need for more generous staffing levels. The telephone lines themselves needed an extra two workers throughout the campaign.

A critical problem was the lack of assured funding. Drinkwise cost £36,000 – more than a small agency would spend in a year. The money was raised in painstaking fashion from local authorities, health authorities, alcohol agencies, trusts, businesses, and the trade. Uncertainty about the budget needed to be contained if the group was to forge ahead with the leading events. The launch in particular needed to look good and the steering group needed to be prepared to spend money and think in an imaginative way.

Recommendations from the evaluation

The need for guaranteed minimum funding is one of a series of recommendations in the evaluation study. Whilst commenting positively on the campaign the evaluation also suggests that:

- There should be better provision for handling the public response to the campaign. There was not a flood of referrals for counselling following Drinkwise as happened in the North-East campaign. There are anyway more services in London. But it is to be hoped that Drinkwise got through to people not yet into problem drinking. There is some limited evidence to support this view from the helpline enquiries, over half of whom had not sought advice about drinking before. However, the demand for information was far greater than anticipated and could have been better organized and monitored.

- The campaign could have been aimed at specific groups rather than the general population. It is questionable whether the budget was sufficient for a broad brush campaign in an area the size of London. A well-known advertising agency suggested a minimum publicity budget of £100,000 for a week's campaign. The television airtime which provided the most spectacular publicity would have cost £500,000 at commercial rates and was provided free.

- Future campaign materials should be piloted. Although there are cheap and cheerful ways of achieving this, the implications of more sophisticated messages is that large-scale finance is required – far beyond the resources of the voluntary sector. This may question the viability of low-cost grass-roots campaigns like Drinkwise but at present there is a great gulf between the desirable and the practical in alcohol education.
- The campaign implicitly took as its target a white, possibly middle-class audience by not sufficiently considering the relevance of the publicity to different groups. The poster featured a white, female disc-jockey and the slogan 'know when to say "when"' is an Anglo-Saxon vernacular. Members of the group found it difficult to make sense of a multi-cultural campaign but, in an area where 16.5 per cent of the population are from ethnic minority groups, it is undeniably vital to do so.
- Evaluation should be built in from the outset. Six months after the campaign finished the HEA produced an excellent critique of the campaign, but it did not attempt to evaluate the effectiveness of messages and it was not able to contribute dynamically to the evolution of the campaign. However, without due care, evaluation can become as expensive as the product itself.

A final assessment of Drinkwise 1986

The question of evaluation leads into a general assessment of Drinkwise 1986. It is, unfortunately, impossible to judge the full effect of the campaign. It had some undeniable value to the agencies themselves. A number of groups broadened their horizons to include prevention work for the first time and if nothing else Drinkwise ensured that treatment and counselling agencies made a splash on prevention in 1986. The campaign also heightened the profile of alcohol issues in a way that was admired by others in the voluntary sector and regular high profile events of this kind would do wonders for alcohol awareness.

It is difficult to know how to judge the response to the campaign. It was comforting to learn from London Weekend Television that the alcohol announcements on television produced a far higher response than similar features on netball the previous week, except that a far smaller proportion of the population play netball than drink excessively! It was exciting when members of staff rushed into the office having spotted a Drinkwise advert on a different underground station. It was good for morale to see alcohol adverts prominently displayed and a relief to know that not all the posters had been concentrated at Cockfosters or Theydon Bois. But the effect of billboard advertising is difficult to judge. The 400 replies to an advert in the London *Evening Standard*, which included a cut-out coupon, produced encouragement to advertise regularly. The sheer volume of enquiries, over 2,000 during the week of the campaign, showed the need of on-going information work, but did they alone justify campaigning activity?

It is accepted that health education campaigns need to be part of a long-term prevention strategy and that public education should form one part of a strategy that includes other policy and prevention initiatives. The lively debate over licensing laws is one such area of activity. Perhaps the most serious reservation about Drinkwise is that it lacked further strategic planning to ensure that the campaign, successful in its own right, did not stand alone. This also raises the question of the need for other similar events in the region and of national co-ordination of public education work. There is a sense that Drinkwise campaigns, for all their activity and achievement, are drops in the ocean. Is this too pessimistic? Perhaps it will be easier to tell when more localities have mounted Drinkwise Campaigns – and evaluated them.

Reference

Drinkwise London 1986: An Evaluation A report by Robin Bunton, May 1987. Research report No. 14, published by the Health Education Authority is available from GLAAS, 91 Charterhouse Street, London, EC1M 6HR. Price £1.00 to include postage and packing.

'Youth Matters': an exhibition for young people

David Arnold

'Youth Matters' was an exhibition organized by the South Bristol Alcohol Forum in April 1987. It developed out of a concern in the South Bristol area that alcohol problems and to a certain degree problems associated with other drugs were on the increase. This article describes the planning and staging of the first event in 1986 and the subsequent 'Youth Matters' exhibition. It is hoped that it may encourage others to organize what are basically very simple but effective events.

The South Bristol Alcohol Forum

The South Bristol Alcohol Forum was set up in 1984 as part of a joint initiative between the Avon Council on Alcohol and Avon social services. For some time concern had been expressed by people working in this part of Bristol over the growing problems associated with alcohol and their effects on the local community. The Forum was established, therefore, in an attempt to identify and focus these concerns, to formulate through the co-operation of various organizations some possible solutions, and, finally, to co-ordinate any subsequent responses and actions. The membership of the Forum included representation from social services, the district health authority, the police, the local education authority, the probation service, voluntary organizations, and the Bristol Alcohol Advisory Centre.

Initially the Forum was a success in that it provided an opportunity for the discussion of issues and the sharing of views and philosophies. During the first year it provided training, and established and developed links and dialogue between the various groups and organizations. However, after this initial phase its members began to be concerned that the Forum had become a talking shop and that not enough was being accomplished. This was leading to a dramatic fall in the attendance at the meetings.

In an attempt to remedy this situation it was decided to set up a publicity sub-committee to look at promoting the existence of the Forum and its potential role in the community. This sub-committee quickly recommended that the

Forum should concentrate upon some specific issue, about which the majority of people were concerned. It was decided that this should be alcohol abuse amongst young people.

This narrowing of the focus of the Forum was well received. During subsequent discussions it was agreed to stage an exhibition which would publicize the alcohol and young people issue and also show the resources and services which were available within the community. Whole-hearted support was given to this suggestion, and a great deal of enthusiasm was expressed.

Info '86: youth and health exhibition

In order to maximize the participation and impact of the exhibition it was decided at a very early stage in the planning of the event that it should not be restricted just to alcohol. An invitation was also extended to groups dealing with illegal drugs and other substances. The aims were to bring together exhibitors from a whole range of agencies and groups that help young people, to raise awareness of the problems of 'substance' abuse, and to identify and advertise the various forms of support available to the community. The target audience was young people and their parents, and those involved in working with young people.

It was thought that a budget of between £500 and £800 would need to be raised in order to stage the exhibition. It was hoped that the top figure could be reached as the Forum wanted to 'think big' and make this an important exhibition. However, very few funds were actually raised. The district health authority was approached but was unable to help. As a result of this the Forum had to turn to the resources available within the group. The exhibition went ahead in April 1986 and despite the lack of finance twenty organizations and groups were represented and approximately two hundred visitors attended.

It was generally felt by the members of the Forum that the exhibition had been a success. However, there was a degree of disappointment with the apparent 'limited' public support. In spite of this all the exhibitors indicated enthusiastic support for the exercise to be repeated. With these requests being made for a similar event next year a letter was circulated to gauge the strength of this support. All those who had exhibited were asked to make comments about the exhibition under the following headings:

- aspects of the exhibition that were considered to be successful;
- aspects that could have been improved;
- whether the organization would be interested in taking part in a future exhibition.

Encouraged by the constructive and mainly positive comments received, the Forum decided to repeat the exhibition in 1987, with the further possibility of making it an annual event. It is perhaps worth noting here that one unintended 'success' of the exhibition was the opportunity for the workers of various organizations exhibiting to meet informally to discuss and share ideas. All the exhibitors underlined the value of this as an exercise in itself.

'Youth Matters': exhibition in South Bristol 1987

Following the experiences of 'Info '86' it was agreed that greater consideration would be given to the planning of the exhibition. It became obvious from an early stage that due to pressures of work and existing commitments the future of the exhibition was going to be the responsibility of a small core of Forum members. In many respects this made the task of planning considerably easier. However, with such a small group, individual responsibility was increased dramatically and this at times led to pressures on time and considerable effort on the part of the members of this group.

In the light of comments from the previous year's exhibitors, a number of changes were made in relation to venue, purpose, publicity, and promotion.

The venue in 1986 was the sports hall in the South Bristol Technical College. The facility was impressive. However, the geographical position of the college was thought to be inappropriate as it is not central to the South Bristol area and presented the problem of an awkward journey. In addition, the fact of the college being an 'academic' institution may have inhibited some potential visitors.

It was suggested that an alternative venue be considered and eventually a youth centre was made available. The youth centre was very central to South Bristol and was obviously a place where young people already had access; consequently it was agreed to stage the exhibition there.

All the groups and organizations who had been invited to exhibit at 'Youth Matters' were given the opportunity to visit the youth centre, meet the organizers, and iron out any concerns felt about the event. It was agreed at this meeting that each exhibitor would be asked to contribute £2.00. This was a small but valuable source of income and contributed to the costs of posting the publicity materials.

The purpose of the event was now to inform young people about the resources available to *them* in *their* community, focusing on youth and health-related issues. It was to be an information exchange but with the emphasis on activity and participation. The exhibitors were encouraged to involve people as far as possible in the events of the day, rather than simply displaying posters and leaflets. Consequently videos were shown, educational games were available, including a 'buzzer board' that indicated correct or incorrect responses to a series of questions, and breath-testing was explained by the police and demonstrated on a number of individuals. This all went towards making the 'experience' as active and exciting as possible.

Publicity and promotion are crucial contributory factors to the success of any project of this kind. A criticism of the previous exhibition was the lack of targeted and appropriate publicity. This was perhaps not surprising considering the lack of success in securing money for this purpose. Considerable thought was therefore put into the advertising of 'Youth Matters'. A graphic artist was employed to produce an attractive eye-catching poster which would appeal to young people. At £30 this was a very cost-effective investment. Two thousand of these posters were subsequently printed and circulated throughout the South Bristol area, with a covering letter from the Forum. The coverage was comprehensive and included all secondary schools and colleges, every health centre and GP surgery, every youth club, libraries, supermarkets, police stations, county and city councillors, and local community associations. Through the members of the Forum articles appeared in internal journals and magazines of the organizations represented. A press release was issued to local newspapers and radio stations and a number of features appeared before the event.

The day of the exhibition

'Youth Matters' was officially opened by the Mayor of Bristol. There were 26 exhibitors and over 300 people attended throughout the afternoon and evening. The exhibitors included groups such as Action Sport South West, Hartcliffe and Withywood Detached Youth Project, the South Bristol Alcohol Advice Centre, the local health authority and community health council, and the Road Safety Service, plus a host of local voluntary and community groups. An encouraging aspect of the exhibition was the active involvement of the young people who attended. This was a demonstration of its success, and the exhibition certainly looked and felt both lively and fun. Popular activities were weight-training, sampling non-alcoholic cocktails and drinks, and demonstrations of the breathalyser by the police.

'Youth Matters' certainly had developed and improved from the previous year. However, there were still areas which could have been improved. For example, even though a map was reproduced as part of the publicity poster, it was an oversight that there was no real promotion of the event on the exterior of the youth centre. A guide to the exhibition was produced at the last moment, consisting of a plan of the youth centre and a list of the participating organizations and groups. It was felt that much more could have been made of this. Finally as a large number of the people attending were from schools it might have been worthwhile to produce a simple worksheet which could have been used as a guide round the exhibition, focusing on certain important aspects, and underlining the real purpose of the event.

Concluding comment

Without any formal evaluation of the whole project the comments and conclusions that follow are mainly subjective observations. Obviously the planning of any event is crucial to its smooth running. Having a framework from the 1986 exhibition enabled 'Youth Matters' to build on previous good practice. A valuable lesson learned was the need to create the right atmosphere to encourage young people to attend. This was achieved to some degree by paying attention to small but vital details. The title, the publicity, and the venue are perhaps all good examples of this.

The two exhibitions were organized with virtually no funds. When we were planning the first exhibition this was considered to be a big disadvantage. However, we now feel that this is one of the strengths of the event although, of course, there were still the hidden costs. This is where the Forum being the planning group proved most useful. For 'Youth Matters' the Youth Service provided the venue, the district health authority printed the publicity posters, the Alcohol Advisory Centre provided the postage, the stationery, and the non-alcoholic drinks, and all the Forum members gave their time.

Another important aspect was gaining the support and involvement of local schools and colleges. Many provided minibuses to transport groups of pupils on the day. One school brought two pupils from every tutor group in the school to the exhibition. These pairs of representatives collected information and materials and 'reported back' to their tutor groups. It was extremely encouraging for the Forum to receive such enthusiastic support for the event.

The benefits of an exhibition such as 'Youth Matters' are many and varied. Firstly it can be used to raise issues and provide information. It can also emphasize the amount of support that is available from groups and organizations within the community and encourage the effective use of it. Finally it can demonstrate the co-operation that exists between local groups and further the process of communication and understanding. The Forum could be criticized by some people for using an exhibition such as this as an 'educational' event. 'Youth Matters' never set out to be education on alcohol and drugs but rather a way of raising issues, and focusing attention on the work already being carried out in the South Bristol area. It is hoped that it was able to achieve this.

It has been made clear from the support given that this type of event is very welcome. In many respects 'Youth Matters' now has a life of its own independent of the South Bristol Alcohol Forum. That is very positive. It is after all a very simple idea, and one that can easily be reproduced. Perhaps the best indicator of its success is that the idea is spreading. A planning group in Weston-super-Mare has been formed and is now planning to stage a 'Youth Matters' exhibition for *its* young people.

Relations with the local media

Peter Rørstad

In 1975 the then North-East Council on Alcoholism (NECA) took responsibility for the local management of the then Health Education Council's experimental 'sensible drinking' campaigns which ran for the following twelve years. This involvement had a radical impact on NECA in many ways, of which one was the gradual development of a close and productive working relationship with various aspects of the local media.

Managing the campaign meant taking responsibility for:

- production and control of the budget provided by the HEC for the maintenance of local alcohol education initiatives;
- acting as the focal point for interest arising from the media campaign;
- acting as a local spokesperson on campaign issues;
- arrangement of all local education and training events in co-operation with local health education units;
- provision of a secretariat to a regional committee set up to plan local developments in support of the media campaigns.

All this established NECA as an authoritative source of expertise, advice, and information both for the media and for the watching, listening, and reading public. In addition, it produced close links between the Council and the expanding network of local NHS education units.

At an early stage in the HEC campaign we recognized that there were significant disparities of language and perception of drinking problems between the press and the 'alcohologists'. This was in part resolved by running a training day for journalists in which we examined some of the more prevalent myths and labels related to drinking behaviour. The day was run as a press briefing, and resource packs were provided. The packs were designed to attract the interest of journalists whilst increasing their awareness of some language of and issues around problem drinking. The contents included factual leaflets, a list of all local agencies in the North-East, a balloon (to humorously highlight the breathalyser test), a sweet (a Polo mint to sweeten the breath after alcohol), a list of 'old style' words together with a list of 'new style' words, e.g. 'alcoholic' should now be referred to as 'problem drinker', and the initial *That's the Limit* leaflet.

Proactive work was felt to be particularly important, so we approached the local commercial television station to suggest that they should produce some documentary work on drinking. They agreed. Subsequently, peak time, five-minute documentaries on various aspects of drinking, including drinking and pregnancy, alcohol and women, and alcohol and young people, were broadcast. It was recognized that programmes of this nature would produce demands for both information and help with problems. In anticipation of this a booklet was produced. This was designed in consultation with and funded by the television company. It was distributed on demand. The concept and title of the booklet, *That's the Limit*, were both used at a later date by the BBC in its national campaign, run in conjunction with the Health Education Council.

The frequency and quality of contact with commercial television has had numerous benefits to all concerned. NECA:

- has acted in a consultancy capacity on the development of several documentary programmes on substance abuse, and on aspects of the development of a workplace policy for the company;
- has participated in numerous news, documentary, and 'entertainment' programmes over the years;
- has been allowed to use the film material produced in its own promotional and training videos.

Other examples of the quality of the relationship between the Council and the television company include the co-option of a member of the Tyne Tees TV (TTTV) staff on to the Council's education and training committee, and the appointment of a member of NECA staff to the central management committee of the Public Service Announcement (PSA) service in the North-East. As a direct result of this TTTV runs training events for the voluntary sector on media presentation and style. Co-operation has recently been extended to include the filming of an episode of *Supergran* at NECA head office – for an appropriate fee!

The methods of conducting business with TTTV have varied according to need but have included consultation with producers and researchers, and the use of small working groups. To date there have been comparatively few problems. However, there are two realities which have had to be dealt with by the Council:

the need to accept that the media are in the business of entertainment and therefore anything which will not be of interest to significant numbers of viewers will not be given air time;

the fact that the nature of the media is such that priorities for screening can change from minute to minute.

Frustration with media colleagues for not using material which has been produced, or for altering schedules at the last minute, is counter-productive in maintaining a good working relationship. For the voluntary sector to use the media appropriately it is necessary for it to think as the media think. This is achieved only over time and from maintaining a dialogue with both journalists and programme producers.

The key to understanding NECA's perspective is to recognize the need for total flexibility in the timing and content of programmes, and also to accept that what is of considerable interest and importance to you may not contain anything that is of sufficient excitement to attract public and, therefore, media attention. The implications for this in terms of strategic planning are significant. Where an event is likely to be of interest to the media they may find it valuable to have either substantial advance notice of it in order to slot an item into a news or current events programme, or alternatively to be offered sole access to the event.

In parallel with the developing relationship with television has been a wide range of contacts with local radio and press, which have been pursued along the same lines. Council staff have participated regularly in phone-ins and feature programmes on local radio, have advised on the planning of a 'theme-week' entitled 'Action Special 19+' (a Radio 1 broadcast), and taken part in the associated broadcasts. 'Action Special 19+' was broadcast over a period of one week and encouraged people to phone in with problems of a generic nature such as housing, welfare rights, unemployment, and alcohol/drug addiction. NECA provided a team of voluntary counsellors to handle the alcohol/drug problems. In addition to regular contact with local radio on news items, the Council now has a standing invitation to advise on any topics that should be given consideration 'on the air'.

Press contacts have been developed over the years to produce a similar balance of reaction and proaction. The effect of this is seen in extremely frequent requests for comment on news items relating to substance abuse, in the publication of a series of articles based on the work of the Council, and extending into the work of the other regional agencies. The additional benefits which have accrued include publicity for NECA services and for its fund raising, and advice to the Council on the development of its public image.

The key elements of the NECA's relationship now with the media are:

- the education of the media, including:
  - offers of participation in training
  - reiteration of themes, e.g. alcoholism *v* problem drinking
  - provision of literature

- co-operation with the media:
  - by being readily available for news comment
  - through participation in planning groups
  - through acceptance of media constraints
  - in production of literature
- proactive work through suggesting themes:
  - for documentaries
  - for news
  - for investigative features
- press briefings:
  - to an updated list of press contacts
  - to individual journalists on specific topics
  - to local newspapers on local issues
- approaching the media as employers:
  - to advise on workplace policies
  - to offer counselling services
  - to offer educational material

NECA's relationship with the media has evolved rather than been created through a system of strategic planning. Nevertheless, it is clear that the voluntary sector has much to offer the media and vice versa. In fact, the system that has evolved contains many parallels with the marketing methods used in a more dynamic and hard-headed way by commercial concerns. In conclusion NECA's experience suggests that there is much to be gained from the conscious creation of close collaboration with all the local media at levels beyond the mere production of news and items of topical concern.

'Winabike': an approach to alcohol education for teenagers

Ken Painter

Young people were identified as a major priority in the South-West 'Understanding Alcohol' Programme. We were anxious to try an innovative approach to dealing with a target audience which appears particularly unresponsive to straightforward health education messages. The idea of a competition which offered an expensive and attractive prize for the creation of a message *for* teenagers *by* teenagers sprang from this and was warmly supported by the Health Education Council (HEC), who provided the necessary funding through the South-West Programme. This article describes the way we approached alcohol education with teenage motorcyclists in an attempt to create messages that the target group could identify with.

From the start, the project was conceived as a joint endeavour, involving the voluntary sector (the Avon Council on Alcoholism), the statutory sector (Southmead health authority's health education department), commerce and industry – who were to be invited to donate prizes towards the competition. From the very start we sought and were given the support of the Avon youth service, the county Road Safety Department, and the Avon and Somerset Constabulary. These organizations did more than lend their names. They all readily provided information on request and each took an active part in distributing the competition material. Their help and encouragement is gratefully acknowledged.

At our first formal planning meeting, the basic format of the competition was agreed. We would organize a competition to win a motorcycle suitable for a young teenager. The contest itself would involve answering ten questions, five on alcohol and five on basic roadcraft. There would be a 'tiebreaker' question, which would require the entrant to contribute an idea that would cut down drinking and driving amongst teenage motorcyclists. We were careful not to inhibit any possible approaches to the tiebreaker and, as will be described later, we received a wide selection of suggestions.

All of the motorcycle manufacturers, importers, and local dealers were asked if they would like to donate a motorcycle or, failing that, to provide one at a concessionary rate. The Honda Company generously agreed to co-operate. At the same time, letters were sent to over seventy local and national organizations, seeking minor prizes or cash donations towards the competition and twenty-two separate prizes were found in this way.

We had decided beforehand that, provided a learner motorcycle could be purchased from the funds awarded by the HEC, we would run the competition, using the balance of the £2,000 grant to meet the administrative and promotional costs. If necessary the grant would be supplemented from our departmental budgets. This proved unnecessary. Honda at first agreed to provide a £1,700 motorcycle for a nominal sum of £500, but later they offered to donate it, completely free of charge: a very welcome and generous gesture. The high number and the value of the remainder of the prizes was also very welcome. This meant that virtually the whole of the HEC grant could be used to produce top quality entry forms and publicity materials, with a small amount going on administrative costs – mainly postage expenses.

The county Road Safety Officer helpfully provided a selection of questions based on the Highway Code and I had the task of providing a selection based on the HEC publication *That's the Limit*. The final selection of five questions from each was then made by the organizers and their selection was endorsed by the local Drink Drive Forum, who also agreed to provide the judges for the contest. The ten statements which had to be judged 'true' or 'false' were:

- A half pint of beer and a single measure of spirits contain the same amount of alcohol.
- The minimum tread depth on a motorcycle tyre is 1 mm.
- It takes two hours for the body to get rid of the alcohol in half a pint of beer.
- The Highway Code advises that you look behind before overtaking unless your machine is fitted with mirrors.
- Your exhaust system, not just your silencer on your bike, must be in efficient working order.
- Road accidents after drinking are the biggest cause of deaths in young men.
- As you reach traffic lights, they are showing amber. Red will be next.
- One in three of the drivers killed in road accidents is over the legal limit of alcohol.
- The advice to drivers turning left to look out for cyclists or motorcyclists coming up on your left is not in the Highway Code.
- Alcohol is a stimulant.

Southmead health education department is fortunate to employ a highly talented graphic designer and she was asked to design an eyecatching competition entry form. Her finished design proved to be extremely popular, attracted much favourable comment, and was, in itself, a powerful inducement to the organizations who agreed to distribute it.

At a fairly late stage in the design of the entry form, a local driving school offered to provide a free driving lesson to each entrant. This seemed to be a kind-hearted gesture as it meant that we could say with some truth that the contest was one in which every entrant would receive a prize! In practice it caused an enormous amount of ill feeling amongst the motorcycle trade, many of whom saw it as a thinly disguised attack on motorcycling itself. A large local dealer withdrew his support as a result of this and nothing we could say or do would persuade him to promote the competition. On balance, it was a mistake to accept the driving school's offer, which was made with the best of intentions. Only four entrants took up the offer and we learned our first lesson the hard way: keep the focus clearly on the target group and do not allow rival interests to become involved!

Distribution of the entry forms was to be through motorcycle dealers, youth clubs, libraries, secondary schools, sports centres, health centres, and any other venues that teenagers frequented. We hoped to utilize the internal mailing systems of the 'institutional' services as much as possible, but here we encountered some irritating bottlenecks. All too often, individuals within these organizations would offer to act as a central distribution point, but would simply not move on the entry forms and posters as agreed. The one honourable exception to this was the library service. They distributed hundreds of the entry forms so that they were available in every library in the county. Another valuable lesson was learned from this: it is much better to distribute the material direct to the point of display.

Press releases were sent out and the media responded very positively, with good free publicity in the local press. In addition, HTV West in Bristol chose to produce a programme on the problems of young people and alcohol. John Teller and I took part and discussed the forthcoming competition. As is often the case, we would have preferred the programme to focus more on the positive things we were attempting, rather than the problems as they saw them, but even so the publicity was very useful.

Approximately 14,000 entry forms were distributed, with another 500 used as publicity leaflets. But, as mentioned above, not all of the leaflets or posters were displayed and some reached their intended display point after the start of the competition itself, when the impetus gained from the initial publicity had died down. The county Road Safety Officer had advised us that, on average, 5,000 applications for provisional motorcycle licences were made annually, so it was felt that our print run of 15,000 was about right. As will be detailed below, we finally received 80 entrants for the competition. Comparison with colleagues who have run large-scale competitions elsewhere suggests that the response rate was as high as can normally be expected from this style of promotion.

We were anxious to keep as high a media profile as possible during the life of the competition, so we issued a series of press releases throughout the period. The first press release was embargoed until the start date of the competition. It received good publicity in all of the local papers and on both local radio networks. The offer of additional prizes from sponsors who had not responded earlier gave the opportunity for further publicity half way through the competition period and more again just before the closing date, which brought a final flurry of entries.

The competition itself ran for four months. Shortly after the closing date the entries were examined and the few with incorrect answers were eliminated. We had wanted to encourage a wide variety of responses and were greatly impressed by many of the imaginative tiebreaker answers. We received suggestions for posters, catchy slogans, poems, a pop song, suggestions for changes in the law regarding drinking and young people, and suggestions for modifications to motorcycles to make the rider more aware of the risks of drinking and driving. The eligible entries were then displayed to the judging panel from the Avon Drink Drive Forum and the winners selected.

The winner was 18-year-old Laurence Jenkins who had submitted a design for a poster, with the selection of two suitable messages. His winning design was printed, and now forms part of the stock of educational and promotional materials provided by the Avon Council on Alcoholism. It has proved to be a popular and effective item and brisk sales to other organizations suggest that other health educators share our enthusiasm for it.

Laurence was presented with his prize on 29 April 1987 by the Chief Constable of the Avon and Somerset Constabulary, Mr Ronald F. Broome, OBE. He received a new Honda MTX125R motorcycle, donated by Honda (UK) Ltd, a year's free insurance donated by the Norwich Union Insurance Group, and a place on the Gold Star, Star Rider's Scheme, donated by Star Riders. In addition he was awarded a crash helmet, a riding suit, a motorcycle jacket, a pair of motorcycle boots and gloves, a safety vest, a maintenance kit, and a full service and safety check of the machine. All of these items were donated as prizes and the organizers provided one year's excise licence for the motorcycle. The decision to equip the first prize winner 'from head to toe' was made by the organizers once the full list of prizes was known. We were conscious of the need to ensure that our prize winner was not put to any unnecessary risk as a result of the competition! It should also be stressed that, although our prize winner was 18 years old, we quietly contacted his parents before he was notified of his award and gained their support.

Runners-up received a total of eleven other prizes, all donated by sponsors, both local and national. We were surprised and disappointed to find that the local press did not turn up at the prize-giving ceremony itself, but were gratified to find that the event was well reported as a result of the press release that had been circulated before the event. BBC Radio Bristol featured Laurence in an exclusive interview immediately after the award ceremony and made motorcycling, alcohol, and road safety the theme of their phone-in programme for the rest of the day. This additional publicity was both unexpected and very welcome and listeners to the programme clearly welcomed the initiative we had taken.

In conclusion, the idea of the competition to raise awareness among young motorcyclists proved to be a good one. With the generous help of the HEC we were able to guarantee that the competition was visible and this enabled us to attract some high value sponsorship from both national and local organizations. We made some elementary mistakes, but we were able to overcome them without endangering the competition itself. For some three months, the issue of teenage motorcyclists' safety was firmly in the media spotlight in Avon, the multi-agency approach worked well, and has continued to benefit those involved even after the end of the contest. We acknowledge that we are fortunate in Bristol in having two television stations, two highly successful local radio channels, and a popular, well respected and high quality local newspaper. Their help and co-operation played a significant part in the success of the competition, but, even without all these 'built-in' advantages, we feel that the idea could profitably be replicated in other parts of the country.

Alcohol and licensed premises

Introduction

The five chapters in this section deal with a number of important liquor licensing issues. The liquor licensing laws are intended to control the number, type, and distribution of alcohol retail outlets in a locality and ensure that licensed premises are both structurally adequate and properly managed. Licensing magistrates in each locality have absolute discretion to grant or withhold most types of licence and applicants for licences must satisfy the magistrates that they are 'fit and proper' people and that their premises meet all the appropriate health and safety standards.

In practice, however, the liquor licensing laws in the UK are far from being the formidable battery of local controls over availability which they appear to be on paper. Whilst magistrates do have the right to grant or withhold licences on the basis of local 'need', this elusive concept is difficult to define and defend. How many outlets are 'enough' and why will one more (or two more, or three more) make any difference? These are questions that are always asked when appeals are heard against decisions to refuse a licence. Because they are difficult to answer, few such appeals fail unless clear-cut issues of public annoyance are involved. As a result, many local licensing committees have abandoned the unequal struggle with determined commercial forces. Providing basic criteria are satisfied, licences are usually routinely granted and ultimate decisions about 'need' are left to market forces.

The core of the problem is that magistrates must consider every application 'on its merits' and not judge it by reference to an overall view as to the number, type, or distribution of outlets in their locality. Thus, although a number of licensing committees now have licensing policies, these tend to focus on important but comparatively routine procedural issues and make, at best, only the vaguest of statements on strategic matters. Yet, as the experience of some localities proves, the 'case by case' erosion of magistrates' discretion can be arrested. Determined committees, armed with well-considered views and information on the nature and extent of alcohol-related problems in their localities, can make their decisions 'stick'. A few localities have even begun to incorporate their strategic views on what constitutes a desirable pattern of licensing development into policies. These make it clear that applications will not be routinely measured against the statements in the policy about number, type, and distribution of outlet and that every application will be judged on its merits. However, they stress that the onus is on the applicants to demonstrate the special merits of their application and thus show why, all other things being equal, an exception should be made in their case.

The first two chapters in this section go to the heart of these central licensing issues. Mr Bernard Miller is a former chairman of the Sheffield licensing committee. His was one of the very first licensing committees in the country to seek to develop systematic contacts with local agencies other than the police, such as the probation service, the trade, social services, public transport, and neighbouring licensing committees, in an attempt to acquire useful information and to develop a consistent, widely publicized, and defensible liquor licensing strategy. As his chapter makes clear, the Sheffield licensing forum has encountered some difficulties. Colleagues on other benches, under great pressure themselves, have been reluctant to share the organizational burden. Forum discussions have sometimes tended to focus less on licensing issues than on participants' own parochial preoccupations, but these are minor problems compared with the major achievement of making licensing issues in Sheffield a community concern.

In talking to many groups and listening to what they have to say about licensing-related problems, Bernard Miller and his colleagues are not 'taking instructions' or sacrificing one jot or tittle of their discretion or duty to act impartially. On the contrary, by becoming better informed and more aware of the wide-ranging implications of their decisions and the many factors which ought to inform them, they are able to use their discretionary powers more appropriately. Unfortunately, many licensing committees do tend to see contacts of the kind being forged in Sheffield as circumscribing discretion and as an opportunity for the exercise of improper influence. Sadly, this appears to have been the case in the second chapter which outlines the failure of the licensing forum in Weston-super-Mare. Peter Steel's account of this failure contains some very important lessons for any locality contemplating a forum initiative. Widespread fears and misapprehensions among magistrates will have to be laid before progress can be made.

One way forward may well be to concentrate on the topical issue of licensed premises and violence rather than the major strategic questions concerning number, type, and distribution of outlets which are intimately linked to the sensitive issue of magistrates' discretion. Violence in and around licensed premises is a focused, specific, and highly topical question amenable to a local response. It is clearly a community problem in which a number of local agencies are likely to have an interest, a view, and something to contribute to debate. John Stevenson, an inspector with Humberside police, is the author of the third chapter in this section. His chapter outlines an attempt to introduce a scheme designed to give early warning of trouble in vulnerable city-centre public houses in Hull and exclude trouble makers from entry to other premises.

Inspector Stevenson outlines the major problems which the scheme encountered and which rendered it, in the event, perhaps less than completely successful. However, many of the initiatives outlined in this book encountered setbacks. The point is to learn from other people's experiences and improve on their experiments. Could a variant of the early warning scheme in Hull work in your city? How would you iron out the snags encountered in Hull?

Deirdre McLean's chapter is also concerned with licensed premises and violence. It focuses on an important aspect of the problem: the contribution that environmental design can make to reducing the likelihood of violence. Her account of how advice on this issue was made available to licensees in the Leicester area in a clear, readable, and practical leaflet is interesting, not least because it involved a close and co-operative effort between the trade and an alcohol agency. She also has some important observations to make on the problems of collecting data on violent incidents connected with licensed premises. These will be of special interest to those planning an initiative in this area.

Both Stevenson and McLean stress overcrowding as a key issue in relation to public houses and violence. Commercial pressures on licensees force them to make sales their overriding priority. These pressures can be particularly acute in city-centre public houses which are often managed, not tenanted. These 'fashion circuit' public houses are thus often severely overcrowded in the evenings when they are patronized virtually exclusively by a young clientele. A local initiative directed specifically at this particular problem would be of inestimable value and interest to other localities. Clearly, much depends upon the brewers, but it is reported that there are local controls over public house numbers which could be enforced if agencies such as the fire service, environmental health departments, the police, and the magistrates were prepared to co-operate in their systematic implementation and enforcement. At least, a clear summary of which organizations can do what in relation to overcrowding would be welcome. The local organizations likely to be involved often have conflicting views about their powers to regulate numbers in public houses.

The final chapter by Derek Sangster describes an important initiative designed to provide young people with an alcohol-free public house, thus making at least a dent in the all-pervasive drinking culture which underpins the alcohol-related violence experienced by so many cities and towns. The labour of love described in this chapter has been a major success in promoting an alternative lifestyle and underlining the all-important message that alcohol is not a necessary and indispensable adjunct to all social occasions. The initiative has led to the formation of other establishments providing the ambience youngsters seek but without the drink.

All the chapters in this section offer stimulating insights into the kinds of activities and initiatives which can be tackled in the liquor licensing area. Such initiatives are important. Huge amounts of time and energy have recently been expended debating reform of the liquor licensing laws. But these debates have ignored the complex, multi-faceted nature of these laws, and the issues associated with their implementation at the local level. Only local action can address the important questions. It is to be hoped that more initiatives of the kind described in this section will shift the so-called 'reform debate' from peripheral questions to the central licensing issues.

A licensing forum

Bernard Miller

In March 1984, the Sheffield licensing committee invited colleagues from four neighbouring jurisdictions in South Yorkshire and North Derbyshire to a joint conference to discuss matters of common interest. The letter of invitation was to the following effect:

> Between us we face many and varied problems in dealing with licensing applications and it would be very helpful to share our experiences and to discuss our respective approaches to common problems.

At that time, Sheffield was in the process of developing certain policies that were more interventionist than had previously applied and it was realized that if these policies were to be effective it would be as well to seek the understanding and support of colleagues from other licensing committees. It had also become apparent in other ways that greater consistency of decision-making within the region was desirable, and the joint conference was thus convened for general discussion; it was chaired by a senior Crown Court judge.

It was the belief of the Sheffield committee that a free-market approach to liquor licensing was inappropriate in current social conditions. Rather, local licensing policies should seek to restrict the indiscriminate spread of licence facilities and ensure, as far as possible, that the control and presentation of alcohol reflected its special nature. The committee's purpose was to contain alcohol abuse and to encourage people to drink sensibly. It was considered that the DHSS discussion document *Drinking Sensibly* (DHSS, 1981) gave general support for this approach.

By coincidence, we were contacted at this time by Philip Tether who was then engaged upon the DHSS research which ultimately led to the publication of *Preventing Alcohol Problems: A Guide to Local Action* (Tether and Robinson, 1986). We had the benefit of a discussion with him and of seeing an initial draft of the report. It was encouraging to us to note that a local licensing forum was to be one of the principal recommendations of the report and the whole rationale of the chapter on licensing in the guide accorded closely with our own thinking. The Sheffield licensing forum thus owes its title but not its origin to the guide.

At the joint conference in March 1984 we had expressed the hope that one of the other committees might be willing, in their turn, to convene another meeting at a future date in order to keep the joint discussions going. In the event, that did not happen and Sheffield decided that they would maintain the initiative and convene a full licensing forum. As a first step, an *ad hoc* meeting of representatives of the police, the probation service, and the medical profession in the locality was called to canvass views. They were encouraging and the first full forum meeting was held on 23 November 1984. The letter of invitation for that meeting read as follows:

> Invitations are being sent to all agencies with an interest in alcohol-related matters, including representatives of the licensed trade (Brewers' Association, Licensed Victuallers' Association and the Off-Licences Association), the police, the fire services, various departments of the local authority, the probation service, the legal and medical professions, Alcohol Concern and magistrates from Sheffield and other licensing districts.
> The purpose of the Forum is to facilitate the exchange of information and opinions upon alcohol-related matters, leading to the development and co-ordination of strategies designed to promote sensible drinking, contain public disorder, and improve social welfare and community health.

The first meeting

There was a good response and some sixty people attended the meeting. Philip Tether gave an opening address and at the conclusion a small steering committee was appointed to arrange for future meetings. The pattern then established has been followed in each of the subsequent meetings, which are held at about six-monthly intervals.

For the meeting held on 20 November 1986 the steering committee decided that the invitation list should be extended to additional licensing committees, and altogether ten committees were represented. The hope was that by this means the forum might become firmly established on a regional basis and that responsibility for organizing and hosting subsequent meetings might be shared on a rotational basis. Sheffield would thus cease to be the focal point with sole responsibility and the forum might become better established as a continuing entity with a momentum of its own. Accordingly the letter of invitation said this:

> The idea of the forum seems to have been generally welcomed and its meetings are well attended. The scope for further talks and discussions, to the benefit of the work of licensing committees, is obviously enormous and it is hoped that such meetings will continue to be held. However, it has to be questioned whether it is desirable for Sheffield to continue to have prime organizational responsibility or whether it would be better for the forum to

take on a regional role perhaps with some form of rotation. If this were to happen then perhaps a permanent executive or steering committee might be established, as now, to maintain continuity.

The final item on the agenda was 'To discuss generally the forum concept and if thought fit to make arrangements for the future meetings.'

In that discussion there was general agreement that further meetings should be held, but no one then present volunteered to become involved. Those who spoke emphasized that they were already fully committed. Such a response, though disappointing, was understandable. Thus it was clear that if the forum was to be continued the onus remained, at least for the time being, with Sheffield.

To sum up, the principal aims of the forum may be said to be to open up lines of communication with others interested in the same field; to debate and achieve a better understanding of licensing issues, and to achieve greater consistency of decision-making. Has anything been achieved so far? In our view it certainly has. We have improved the degree of co-operation locally between ourselves and the various statutory and non-statutory authorities and agencies concerned with the consequences of alcohol misuse, and we have a much closer rapport with our licensing colleagues of other jurisdictions. We believe we also have close contact with the brewing industry and by continuing the debate we should be better informed and better able as licensing justices to fulfil our responsibilities.

The lessons so far

Are there any general lessons to be learned from our experiences to date? Firstly, it is important to emphasize that in organizing a forum meeting, little can be achieved in the course of half a day comprising $2\frac{1}{2}$ hours. The general feeling at our last meeting was that a full day, with lunch provided, would be preferable. This necessitated an apportionment of the cost but it was considered, from the magistrates' point of view, that it was a legitimate training expense. A per capita charge will, of course, have to reflect the fees and expenses which might be payable to invited speakers.

Second, the agenda for the meeting needs to be carefully drawn so as to include items of general interest in the licensing field, and there should be adequate opportunity for a full discussion; fragmentary and indeterminate discussion on a variety of topics must be avoided. In other words, one should resist the temptation to try to do too much. Occasionally there is a quite understandable tendency on the part of some participants to stray from strictly licensing issues into matters such as their funding and relationships with other organizations or the adequacy of alcohol services in the locality. These tendencies must be resisted. The purpose of a licensing forum is to debate, develop, and agree concrete and consistent licensing policies in neighbouring jurisdictions. Practical and specific questions must be addressed. Do we approve of 'Children's Rooms'? Can we encourage more and better training for bar staff in our different areas? How are different committees defining 'need' and why? Discussion must be focused. Careful preparation is therefore necessary by any steering committee.

Apart from periodic forum meetings, we found that there remains a need for separate consultation at local level between the various statutory agencies involved in licensing matters. So far as Sheffield is concerned we have established a joint consultative committee with representatives of the police, the fire service, and the environmental health officers, and we have agreed to meet in December of each year to consider matters of mutual interest. Any particular point that arises can, if need be, be brought to public notice at the ensuing general annual licensing meeting.

The Sheffield licensing forum has proved its worth. However, two important questions remain. Can the forum survive without some arrangement for sharing the work and responsibility and without a small but properly funded executive organization? And assuming the forum does survive how can its effectiveness be improved? In our view it would be of immense help if the discussions could take place within the context of a considered statement from government setting out a national licensing strategy, paying due regard to prevailing social conditions. Local efforts might then be seen as part of a cohesive strategy and become much more meaningful.

References

Department of Health and Social Security (1981) *Drinking Sensibly*, London: HMSO.

Tether, P. and Robinson, D. (1986) *Preventing Alcohol Problems: A Guide to Local Action*, London: Tavistock.

A licensing forum that failed

Peter Steel

Weston-super-Mare is a Victorian seaside resort with a population which is currently about 60,000. It is a popular retirement town, in which 27 per cent of the population are aged 65 years and over. At the same time, it has a large population of young people, many of whose families are newcomers. The town has grown by about 15,000 in the last seven years. Alcohol-related disorder and violence is not uncommon, particularly in the summer. The seasonal mix of holiday and indigenous populations means that there are a much higher number of licensed premises (including six night-clubs) than would ordinarily be demanded, and policing becomes difficult, especially at peak times such as weekends and bank holidays. Located in a traditional cider-producing area, this potent beverage is both cheap and widely available in 5-litre containers which can be bought direct from the many farms engaged in cider-making.

The Weston-super-Mare Forum

Alcohol-related disorder has been a part of the local scene for many years, but in early 1984 the situation had deteriorated to such an extent that it was decided to set up a specific body to co-ordinate a multi-agency response to the problem: the Weston-super-Mare Forum on Alcohol Abuse. The initiative for setting up the Forum came from the probation service and local magistrates who approached the Avon Council on Alcoholism (as it was then known) to assist in its creation. The intention was to bring together representatives of a wide range of groups and organizations in the local community who had an interest in alcohol issues and who, it was hoped, could help find an answer to the growth in the town's alcohol-related disorder. For its inception the group self-consciously sought to discover positive new ways to improve the quality of life in Weston-super-Mare and has strenuously sought to avoid being seen as simply 'anti-alcohol'.

The first step in the Forum's creation was to hold a public meeting to allow people to put forward their ideas and viewpoints. It was made clear to everyone that the Avon Council on Alcoholism was prepared to support and promote the proposed Forum but that, in the last analysis, it was to be a 'community body' and not the property of any single group or organization. This approach probably made the forum concept acceptable to many groups and organizations who would otherwise have been more wary.

The Forum has successfully brought together many different groups and organizations in the locality and has established contact which would otherwise not have been made. The chairman of the magistrates took the chairmanship of the Forum and there are currently representatives from the voluntary sector, schools, police, social services, Alcoholics Anonymous, psychiatric services, and community groups. Attendance at meetings fluctuates from as little as eight or nine up to twenty or more. In the three years since its inception, the Forum has turned its attention to a wide range of alcohol-related issues such as alcohol education in schools and the pattern of treatment services in the locality. It has also helped to organize an alcohol and youth conference. Its original remit was alcohol but this has recently been broadened to include drugs and AIDS. The Forum is a valuable 'umbrella' body facilitating contact and co-ordination on a wide range of issues. One of these is the important topic of liquor licensing.

Liquor licensing

For many years, much discussion has taken place locally about who is responsible for the 'alcohol problem'. Public-house licensees blamed off-licences, off-licences blamed supermarkets, supermarkets remained indifferent to the dispute whilst police blamed licensees. Constructive policy initiatives are scarcely likely to develop in this unhelpful atmosphere so the Forum decided to take the initiative by looking at licensing issues. It examined the geographical spread of licensed premises and found that the highest percentage were to be found around the town centre and sea-front areas. One effect of this is that large numbers of intoxicated people are decanted on to the streets between 11 p.m. and midnight. The Forum also established that the closing times of the night-clubs varied, which meant that the police were kept busy over a long period of time. Getting these basic data together was useful and helped to promote informed debate which previously had been long on anecdote and short on facts. However, the most important of the Forum's preliminary findings was that, with few exceptions, new licences were being granted without much local opposition. The proliferation of licences seemed to the Forum members to be the central issue at the heart of much of the town's alcohol-related disorder and they decided this was the topic on which they should concentrate.

Proliferation of liquor licences

It was decided from the outset that the Forum would not take on the role of actively challenging applications for new licences but that it would try to influence the decision-making processes of local licensing magistrates. The clerk to the licensing magistrates was invited to attend a meeting of the Forum where it was hoped that he would be able to advise on how best to work towards a reduction in new licences. Several members thought that perhaps the best way to do this would be to create a licensing forum composed of members from the Forum proper who could be approached by the licensing magistrates for information and viewpoints which they could then take account of when considering the merits of proposals.

The clerk to the licensing magistrates gave much guidance, advice, and information on the way that licences are granted. However, it soon emerged from the discussions that whilst the licensing magistrates shared the Forum's anxieties and concerns over the proliferation of licences, they felt they had little room for manoeuvre.

Magistrates can refuse to grant a licence if (i) the premises do not meet fire and safety standards, (ii) if the person applying is not 'a fit and proper person' to run licensed premises, and (iii) if there is no 'need' for the proposed outlet. Whilst 'need' seems the most promising ground for refusal, magistrates feel both unhappy and uncertain with this concept which is difficult to operationalize and defend. Attempts to do so usually resulted in their decision being overturned on appeal. As a result, local licensing magistrates felt extremely discouraged and doubted their ability to halt the growth of new licensed premises in the town, even though the link with disorder appeared perfectly clear. The proposal to form a 'mini-forum' devoted solely to licensing issues was felt to be constitutionally inappropriate. The licensing magistrates indicated that whilst such a body could oppose a licence, as could any member of the public, they could not take any more or less notice of its recommendations than those of any other member of the public. Thus, the Forum's special initiative in respect of licensing issues foundered. The number of licensed premises in Weston-super-Mare continues to increase as does associated alcohol-related disorder.

Lessons from failure

The Forum's attempt to come to grips with licensing issues in Weston-super-Mare failed and this failure contains a number of important lessons for other localities. Many magistrates clearly felt that it would be improper to consult with the representatives of other groups and organizations in the shape of a licensing forum. However, magistrates in a number of areas (Sheffield is a prominent example) are prepared to consult widely in order to reach general conclusions about 'need' and other liquor licensing issues, such as the appropriateness of family rooms, the training of licensed bar staff, and late-night transport arrangements. Discussions about these and other issues are entirely proper and do not erode the magistrate's discretion nor their duty to examine each application for a licence on its merits. Rather, they help to identify important licensing issues, clarify magistrates' attitudes towards them, and promote consistent decision-making.

The Weston-super-Mare licensing forum was stillborn because of the magistrates' uncertainties, fears, and misapprehensions. Any attempt to set up a local licensing forum must seek to allay magistrates' worries that their discretion is being usurped, and emphasis should be placed on a forum's potential role as a source of data, education, and information. The purpose of a forum is, it must be stressed, to help magistrates make better-informed decisions and, if necessary, to defend those decisions on appeal. If neighbouring jurisdictions collaborate in the development of a joint licensing forum, magistrates from various areas can develop a well-argued collective licensing strategy. With the spread of communication and understanding, it can succeed.

It is unhelpful to give the impression that the sole purpose of a forum is simply to restrict the numbers of licences. This approach suggests that a licensing forum is, indeed, intending to supplant the magistrates' decision-making discretion. Far better to emphasize that there are many other licensing issues which a proposed licensing forum could begin by examining. These might include a survey of licensing policies from other jurisdictions to establish whether there are any particular issues which a local licensing policy should cover. Another task might be to examine the pattern of late-night, alcohol-related violence in order to see whether there are any public houses which appear to attract trouble because of over-crowding, mismanagement, or lack of police supervision, or to identify the steps that local breweries can take to reduce the violence associated with licensed premises. These and other highly specific questions should be of interest to licensing justices and many other groups and organizations in a locality.

A licensing forum can, as experience elsewhere shows, help to raise these and other issues in a considered and focused way. However, magistrates must be helped to see a licensing forum as an ally, not a threat. Careful arguments will be needed to convince them that such a device can be of great use to them in their important work and that it will, ultimately, help to restore and not erode their decision-making powers.

'Pub Watch': an early warning scheme

John A. Stevenson

This case study is an examination of the origins and developments of the public-house early warning scheme ('Pub Watch') which is currently operating in the centre of Kingston upon Hull. The main city-centre policing area covers one and a half square miles and is made up mostly of commercial property with approximately 11,500 residents. To cater for the large amount of people that come into the city for their entertainment there are over seventy public houses and six licensed clubs, the vast majority of which are confined to a small area in the heart of the city centre.

As a result of an examination of public disorder problems in the city it was found that a high proportion of offences were committed in the small area containing the majority of public houses and mostly during times related to licensing hours. These premises become heavily congested, particularly at weekends, and are frequented by young people. The peak periods for disorder are Thursday, Friday, and Saturday evenings.

It is the fashion for city-centre patrons not to stay in one public house, but instead to visit a number of premises in one evening, perhaps having only a single drink in each. This means that at any one time there are large numbers of people, often intoxicated, walking around the city streets, trying to gain entry to already crowded public houses. This transitional activity means the public disorder problems occurring in one premises can easily be transferred to one or more other premises within a relatively short period of time.

In March 1984, as a result of an escalation of public disorder, the policing strategy of the city centre was changed from one of reaction to one with an emphasis on prevention. This meant the introduction of high visibility policing in problem areas, and opening up of channels of communication with the licensing community to assist with targeting problems and the effective deployment of resources. However, due to the transitional activity it was difficult to prevent disorder. This was because trouble-causers were being ejected from one premises and simply moving to another where once inside problems again developed. As a result of the crowding in the public houses it was often very difficult for the police to gain entry and deal with the problem and it was felt that it would be of great assistance to keep the trouble-makers on the streets where the problems could be resolved more easily.

Developing 'Pub Watch'

The decision was made to develop a form of early warning system between the popular licensed premises in order that a group ejected from or causing trouble at one public house would not gain entry very easily to another. After consultation a chain system was formed whereby a licensee who was having problems could contact the police as normal and the police, as well as dispatching officers to deal with the problem, would, if some form of group movement was likely, inform the premises on either side in the chain. The licensees themselves would then continue to transfer the message around the chain until all parties were informed. If a licensee experienced difficulties in passing a message to the next in the chain it was agreed they would simply move on to the next premises in line. This would ensure that at least a majority of the premises were aware of the problem. In Hull the chain is made up of twenty-four premises.

To introduce the system to the licensees and other bodies involved it was decided to develop a form of licensing forum and to this end all participants were invited to a meeting where the situation, problems, and aims of 'Pub Watch' were discussed. Present at this meeting were the licensees themselves, representatives from their breweries, representatives of the Licensed Victuallers' Association (LVA) and the National Association of Licensed House Managers (NALHM), the superintendent from the covering police sub-division, along with officers from relevant police departments, and Philip Tether from Hull University, who was carrying out research into alcohol and related problems.

The original scheme proposed was discussed and revised, resulting in the system already described which was accepted by all present. It is perhaps obvious that one aspect of the system that would cause landlords some difficulty is actually preventing someone from entering their premises. To this end the scheme was perhaps fortunate in that the majority of the premises do control the flow and behaviour of customers by employing doorstaff. Therefore, all the landlords had to do was to devise a system of getting information received by telephone to the doorstaff at the entrances. As a result of this scheme and liaison with breweries, the premises that did not employ doorstaff began to do so, and thus a form of prevention was immediately introduced.

In the initial meeting opinion was voiced that it would be of assistance if there was some form of legal bar to trouble-causers entering licensed premises. Research showed that it was possible to apply for exclusion orders under the Licensed Premises (Exclusion of Certain Persons) Act, 1980. This Act allows magistrates to make an exclusion order from certain specified premises for any person who has been convicted of an offence of violence within licensed premises. This order can stand for between three months and two years. It was decided that the police prosecutions department would set up a system for applying for such orders in suitable cases. Each licensee agreed that his premises would be one of those specified in future exclusion orders. However, exclusion orders are difficult to police and it was agreed that the general aim should be to try to force out the main ringleaders from the city centre, and not simply apply for an order in every case.

After the initial meeting, details of the scheme were announced in the local press. It was hoped this might help in warning trouble-makers that their activities would not be tolerated. In addition, each premises involved in the scheme was visited by police community liaison officers to clarify any problem areas and to give encouragement to use the scheme. Regular follow-up visits were also made, again with the aim of highlighting and solving any problem areas.

The local police also provided posters on which were printed in black on a dayglo yellow background the following words: 'These premises are part of the "Pub Watch" Early Warning System. Anyone convicted of an offence of violence in these premises is liable to a ban by the Court from public houses in the city centre.' These posters were displayed at prominent points, usually behind the bar.

How successful has 'Pub Watch' been?

How effective has the scheme been? In the past publicity about the articles on public disorder in the local press have produced the effect of escalating trouble. This could be because of 'copycat' behaviour and a general feeling that acceptable levels of behaviour have been lowered. Some increase in disorder was anticipated from the extra media attention given to 'Pub Watch' but this was not the case and problems did not appear to escalate after its introduction. However, major problems were experienced in the simple transference of warning messages from pub to pub. It was found that many public houses do not have telephones behind the bar or in some location that is reasonably quiet so that messages could be heard. Also in some cases premises did not even have a normal telephone, they only had a public pay telephone somewhere in the public part of the premises. This type of equipment causes lots of problems in a system such as this as the machines are often engaged, or messages are difficult to hear, or the person answering the call has no money with which to operate it so that the messages can be passed on.

Another area of difficulty was that premises are located very close to each other in relation to walking distance. Often the trouble-causers had walked to the next premises before the message was received. This caused frustration among licensees and the scheme fell into disrepute among participants. In addition, it was found that in the past a form of unofficial grapevine was operated by some licensees now involved in the scheme. They tended to give priority to their established contacts, thus further slowing down the transference of information. Because some licensees ignored the official chain it became impossible to actually evaluate how much the scheme was being used and how effective it was.

There was also a problem of training, in that licensees had to find time to train their staff as to how the system operated and also how to formulate the information into a form that could be understood and utilized by the receiver in order to avoid the message becoming totally distorted by the end of the chain, which has happened on some occasions. The old story of 'bring-three-and-fourpence-we're-going-to-a-dance' becomes relevant.

However, the overriding problem with the scheme was one of lack of use. It is the type of scheme where information, use, and interest has to be on the whole generated by the licensees themselves and unfortunately it would appear that a general level of apathy prevailed despite being given an opportunity to solve some of their problems. As this scheme has been very little used it has become increasingly difficult to maintain any level of interest, making it even more difficult to make the system work.

Conclusion

Experience in Hull suggests that a successful 'Pub Watch' scheme requires great attention to apparently small details such as the siting of telephones in participating public houses and agreement on the exact details of information to be transmitted from pub to pub by properly trained staff. In addition, the existence of informal communication networks must not be allowed to impede the development of a more comprehensive official 'chain'. Regular review meetings at which the successes and failures of a scheme could be examined might help to discourage informal networks and promote interest in its development.

The lack of commitment shown by licensees to the 'Pub Watch' scheme in Hull is partly due to the unanticipated difficulties which were encountered when it was put into operation. Licensees in city-centre public houses, which have special disorder problems, are under great commercial pressures from their breweries. This can lead to severe overcrowding, the source of much trouble. Licensees have little or no financial leeway or incentive to reduce numbers in their premises, hire more bar staff, and recruit responsible doorkeepers. This latter point is particularly important since, unfortunately, some doorkeepers lack any kind of badge or distinctive clothing, are allowed to drink on duty, and are thus in many cases indistinguishable from the clientele. Until breweries are prepared to relax the commercial pressures on vulnerable public houses and to provide financial assistance to make such things as proper telephone facilities available, 'Pub Watch' schemes, however well-designed, can only have a marginal impact on the growing problem of alcohol-related city-centre disorder.

'Pubs and violence': a handbook for licensees

Deirdre McLean

In May 1987 a 16-page booklet called *Safer Houses – A Handbook for Licensees on Pubs and Violence* was produced by the Leicestershire Community Alcohol Services in conjunction with the Leicester-based brewery, Ind Coope and Allsopp. The idea for writing the booklet came from a meeting called by the National Association of Licensed House Managers (NALHM) to discuss the growing problem of violence in Leicester pubs. Dr Douglas Cameron of the Leicestershire Community Alcohol Services attended this meeting and suggested that, in view of the managers' deep concern, the Community Alcohol Services should take the lead in producing some guidance for licensees. Shortly afterwards, Dr Cameron and I met Tony Wagner, the Ind Coope and Allsopp's tied houses general manager, to discuss this proposal. The idea of the booklet received Tony Wagner's enthusiastic support and he became personally involved in the project giving advice and helping to write and produce the booklet. We also succeeded in interesting the Brewers' Society, who agreed to fund the initial print run of 1,000 copies and have subsequently helped to publicize it.

The booklet

The purpose of the booklet is to offer some guidelines to licensees on how environmental factors influence customers' behaviour in their pubs. Subjects dealt with include decor, colour schemes, music, food, lighting, staff attitudes, and dealing with 'drinking-up' time. These and other subjects are dealt with in a clear and simple way and side-headings, illustrations, and brief checklists help licensees assess the environmental adequacy of their premises. The material in the booklet draws heavily on research evidence presented in *Public Policy and Public Drinking* (Single and Storm, 1985).

The booklet emphasizes that, in normal circumstances, the pub is a safe, social drinking environment with its own built-in safeguards and controls. However, in pubs (as in other places) violent or aggressive behaviour sometimes presents a problem and that whilst environmental modifications are by no means a complete answer, they can help to prevent such incidents. Thus, it emphasizes that care should be taken over the choice of colour schemes, since research by psychologists has shown that bright, strident colours (such as red or orange) are more likely to bring out aggressive feelings in people than soft, warm, or pastel shades (such as blue, green, mauve, or grey) which are reassuring. Other aspects of pub decor should be chosen to reinforce, not contradict, any attempt to induce a tranquil mood through the overall colour scheme. Pubs with pictures of landscapes and wallpaper with repetitive patterns are likely to reinforce the right kind of mood whereas pictures duplicating strenuous activity, such as sporting events, are likely to promote the opposite effect.

The booklet continues by discussing, among other things, why it is preferable to have a balance of mixed musical themes provided at a subdued level rather than strident music of one type; and why furniture layout which encourages small intimate drinking groups is an important feature of good pub design. Particular attention is paid to staff attitudes and the way they handle the all-important 'drinking-up' period. Sudden changes of atmosphere created by staff turning up the lights, turning off the music, shouting, and grabbing half-empty glasses can aggravate customers. The booklet emphasizes that it is important for staff to set customers a good example and that their own drinking habits can set the tone of a public house. This means that licensees and bar staff can help others to drink sensibly by keeping a check on how much, when, and where they drink themselves. The best example is set by licensees and bar staff who do not drink behind the bar.

Further developments

It was originally intended that the booklet would be distributed by local brewers to public houses in Leicestershire and would be used by them in their training programmes for new licensees. However, it has roused much wider interest and several months after its first publication a reprint run of 2,000 was necessary to meet demand. The reprints were funded entirely by Ind Coope and Allsopp. I was asked to speak about the recommendations in the booklet at a 'Keeping Pubs Peaceful' Conference held at the Barbican, organized by the Hotel and Catering Trading Board. Following this, the interest shown by both the media and breweries all over the country has been overwhelming, resulting, among other things, in an article in the *Guardian* and a slot on Radio 1's *Newsbeat*.

As is often the way, one initiative leads to, or suggests, another. Tony Wagner suggested that we should respond positively to the Standing Conference on Crime Prevention's Report on the Prevention of Violence in Licensed Premises (Home Office, 1986). This would be another way of encouraging interest in the topic and help to sustain the successful inter-agency collaboration we had achieved in the locality during Christmas and New Year 1986–7 over the running of a 'Designated Driver Scheme'. We invited representatives from the Leicestershire Police Community Affairs Department, the Licensed Victuallers' Association (LVA), the NAHLM, Leicester city council Environmental Health Departments and breweries with a Leicester interest. We held our first meeting in May 1987 at which the booklet was unveiled. We hope this liaison group will continue to meet to develop a co-ordinated response to the problem of violence on licensed premises.

At the first meeting, it was decided to conduct a survey of violence associated with licensed premises since, although the breweries do ask for a report of each incident from their managers and tenants, very little reliable information was available on a city-wide basis. Unfortunately, the questionnaire has not been a noticeable success. Few incidents were reported. In fact the police confirm that, for reasons no one can explain, the reporting of incidents decreased when licensees were asked to complete the questionnaire. Another problem may have been its length. Licensees who have to fill out a lengthy report form on violent incidents for their own breweries may well be reluctant to complete another for third parties. Efforts are now being made to collect the reliable data we are seeking from other sources. One promising source are the records of in-coming calls to the police. In the past, calls from licensed premises have not been separately 'flagged' and were not distinguishable from other calls that the police receive. However, if these are 'flagged' in some simple way they can be separated out and used to provide a 'map' of violence associated with licensed premises. When we know what we are dealing with, the liaison group will then be able to decide on an appropriate response.

In the meantime, the Leicestershire Community Alcohol Services are developing a parallel initiative designed to make use of data on the pattern of violence once reliable information becomes available. The environmental features of all vulnerable, city-centre public houses in Leicester have been assessed in order to test the connection between such features and levels of disorder. We hope this will give the liaison group solid material to inform its deliberations and help us to refine our advice on environmental safety in public houses.

Conclusion

The booklet on environmental safety was a great success because it was practical, simple, and direct. Moreover, it was enthusiastically supported by a local brewery, one of whose directors became deeply committed to the project. Ind Coope and Allsopp have consistently supported the Leicestershire Community Alcohol Services in the promotion both of the booklet and the liaison group. They realize that, at the end of the day, escalating levels of violence associated with licensed premises is bad both for public relations and for business. Whether other breweries in other areas are ready to become so deeply involved in this issue is something you must establish. Unfortunately, the main concern of some breweries appears to be profit rather than the safety and comfort of customers and, if alcohol-related violence is to be tackled, some at least of the former may have to be sacrificed in order to promote the latter. The root of the violence problem in many public houses appears to be overcrowding and, until this basic, environmental question is resolved, the other environmental improvements we suggest stand little chance of influencing behaviour. Nevertheless, our experience in Leicestershire shows that with goodwill and good liaison it is possible for agencies in the alcohol field and the trade to co-operate in the development of prevention initiatives.

The booklet was, perhaps, better received by the brewery than by the licensees themselves. It was very much a 'top down' exercise starting, as I have explained, from discussions between the Leicestershire Community Alcohol Services and Tony Wagner. If I were carrying out the exercise again, I would involve licensees, through the LVA and the NALHM, at a much earlier stage and I would urge anyone engaged in this kind of exercise to approach it from the 'bottom up'. Licensees have a wealth of knowledge and experience to contribute and local alcohol agencies should try to draw on it and include them in their projects. Disorder associated with licensed premises is an important and topical subject and it must come at the top of any locality's licensing forum agenda. However, as the Leicester experience shows, hard data (as opposed to anecdotal evidence and newspaper reports) may be hard to come by. Anyone trying to collect information on which to base licensing forum discussions will probably find it best to seek such data from the breweries themselves or, as in Leicester, to approach the police to see what information is routinely collected and whether small changes in procedure might yield useful material.

References

Home Office (1986) Standing Conference on Crime Prevention, *The Prevention of Violence Associated with Licensed Premises*, London: Report of Working Group.

Single, E. and Storm, T. (eds) (1985) *Public Policy and Public Drinking*, Toronto: Addiction Research Foundation.

The Parrot and Palm idea

Derek Sangster

As a youth worker at a Worthing youth centre, Tim Mason was into the usual fund-raising-and-organizing-activities routine, coping with tatty premises and realizing that even the youngest attenders were already drinking beer and spirits. For young people, pubs and night-clubs are very attractive because of the comfortable, softly-lit rooms and sophisticated atmosphere – not primarily because of the drinks that are served. But where else could they go? There had to be an alternative. This alternative had to be attractive and also alcohol-free (fun doesn't depend on booze); a caring place (to help with problems); a place where people would make good relationships (social education); separate from any youth centre (to avoid the 'youth club' label).

When Tim Mason floated the idea he got good support from teenagers and encouragement from a number of responsible people. Letters were written to many local firms and all local churches asking for support (no response). The best results came from known contacts whose interest was aroused. The hunt for suitable premises was on and a ground-floor shop not far from the town centre owned by a sympathetic businessman came up.

That was the good news. The bad news was that a number of influential people withdrew their support. It seemed that they had begun to realize that the idea was now a serious long-term project and they doubted the feasibility of any club or meeting place which did not serve alcohol. This struggle with the social norm was to be repeated many times.

Setting up the club

The aim was to create a club for the 14 to 21 age group with a sophisticated night-club atmosphere and music and dance-floor lighting to equal any of the competition. The premises were drab, partitioned, and decorated in black and white with a cement floor. Financial resources were nil, but leadership and enthusiasm were there. Tim and fourteen young people set out to win the battle, raise funds, and build the basics.

This way young people were involved from the start raising money and helping in the construction and decoration of their club. Would they have had the same satisfaction and sense of responsibility if it had all been done for them and handed to them on a plate? Four months later the Parrot and Palm Club opened in June 1984 and fourteen young people turned up. Music and lighting were adequate but nowhere near commercial standards, the bar still looked like a kitchen but worked well with supplies and cocktail recipes from Leisure Drinks of Derby. Two days before opening there was no cash – not even enough to buy glasses for the bar. Rescue came from a local voluntary organization.

With a painted floor, palm-tree decor, plastic parrots hanging from the ceiling, and rubber and cheese plants softening the hard lines of the walls, the Parrot and Palm opened two evenings a week, one for a disco, the other for maintenance work. A two-tier membership was established under which guests could attend on two evenings before becoming associate members. Those willing to help could be elected full members. The help areas were catering, cleaning, bar staff, entertainment (i.e. DJs), fund-raising, maintenance, and improvements. Today guests pay £1.50 at the door, associate members £1.00 a year and £2.00 at the door, full members £2.00 a year and 50p at the door. Maintenance and improvement had its own spin-off keeping up attendance and attracting new members as month by month new things appeared like a bar canopy, a decorative fountain, new lighting, and music centre additions. Members could see that their money was being used on improvements.

The Parrot and Palm successes

The big attraction of the Parrot and Palm was the friendly atmosphere – rather like a good party. One member said she would not be ashamed to come to the club in floods of tears because she knew she would get help. With voluntary helpers (always in short supply) the club is a caring concern. Most young people have problems which they find difficult to discuss at home or elsewhere and often these problems are shared with adult helpers. However, not all problems come to supervisory staff – many are sorted out by the young people themselves.

By the spring of 1985, membership had grown to eighty-five and serious consideration had to be given to bringing the premises up to the required standards for health and fire safety. At one point it looked as if the club might have to close down for lack of funds to meet £10,000 worth of construction work, but the members worked hard at fund-raising, writing letters to the press and to councillors. In the end public response enabled it all to be paid for – including the cost of a vinyl dance floor and carpeting. After three months the club reopened for two disco evenings a week (later three) and membership increased rapidly to 500. On some nights people had to be turned away at the door because the then safe maximum of 150 had been reached.

Others heard of this alcohol-free club in Worthing and Tim Mason had to spend a good deal of time visiting and spreading the good news that they could start up similar clubs. There were television and radio interviews and three small caravans were converted into portable bars for outside events (Parrot-vans). In the end Tim was presented with a borough council award for providing Worthing with so much national publicity.

If all this sounds like a too-good fairy tale you can be sure that there were troubles. Tim decided to leave the Youth Service in May 1986 and later that year an attempt was made to run the club and the development work in other places on a commercial basis. It did not work; cash got in the way of caring, and were it not for a rescue operation by Worthing churches led by the Bishop of Horsham the whole system would have closed down by the end of 1986. One result of this was the formation of the Parrot and Palm Development Agency with Tim as director, in January 1987. This put the development of the Parrot and Palm idea in other parts of the country on a sound basis and the clubs at Ealing and Horsham are a direct result of the agency assisting and enthusing hard-working local groups.

Voluntary workers, mostly from the churches, help in the club. But they are difficult to recruit. Many adults have a suspicious fear of the younger generation. Few realize how welcome they are with their skills and experience. Besides supervisory work on a disco night, adults are needed to direct DIY maintenance and reconstruction work. Financially, the door and bar takings keep the club in business but funds have to be raised for major refurbishing and refitting to keep up with the competition. The music system and dance floor lighting fitted in 1985 is first class and is insured for £8,000. There is no shortage of DJs but good ones are worth keeping and encouraging as they can do much to set the tone for the evening. All insurance is done through Ansvar which specializes in non-alcoholic policies, and because of this the club owns a breathalyser to help check that people do not bring alcohol in 'internally'. It is, in fact, seldom used but its presence is helpful.

A police superintendent who came to see the club recalled the discipline he had come to appreciate when a boy in the Sea Cadets with the suggestion that perhaps clubs like the Parrot and Palm lacked this behavioural backbone. He was then shown that the Parrot and Palm has a strong disciplinary structure which is supported by the club peer group – no smuggled-in alcohol, smoking in the dance area only, no aggro. Besides dancing, laughing, chatting, teasing, and enjoying themselves, members like kissing and cuddling too. Even here there is an accepted standard, and the worst punishment for any offence is to be banned from the club for a period. It is interesting that the most enjoyable evenings are usually those when several voluntary helpers are present. Members appreciate the security this ensures. When a young person comes up with a problem it often has its origin with the family at home, and when this is followed up parents are usually very grateful.

Lessons from the Parrot and Palm

For anyone setting up a Parrot and Palm Club the first objective must be to harness the enthusiasm of a group of young people and link them with the adult committee. 'Twinning' young and older members works well while a group in their early twenties can combine enthusiasm with practical know-how and leadership. When fund raising, try hard to get long-term sponsorship rather than donations. Sometimes a handsome donation can suggest to the donor that he or the group have done their bit and should not be approached again. Any committee should contact local churches; although not usually affluent, churches have in their membership many caring people and church policy is usually community-friendly and problem-solving.

When constructing the club use durable materials – half-inch chipboard instead of plasterboard, for instance. Remember too that you may want to alter things later, so it is best to avoid brickwork. Have a good door kiosk or counter to control entry and a bright illuminated noticeboard. Toilets (with a remote lighting switch) must be easy to clean. The club will need its own tools and DIY supervisor. Lighting and music need an electrical supervisor too. Brewery companies are often very generous in donating old furniture from recently refurbished pubs. You will need to fulfil all the conditions required for a public entertainments licence.

The bar needs supervision to see that service and cleanliness is of a high standard; make sure too that a club cleaning team is ready to operate at closing time. The door is a very important area – a welcoming point for members and guests, a barrier for trouble-makers. Make sure that no one who has been drinking enters – a breathalyser can be useful here. Check too on the smuggling-in of alcohol, especially in the toilets which anyway need general surveillance. Make sure new people get introduced to members. A 'No Re-entry' system prevents young people nipping out to a pub and returning; if used ensure the strictest enforcement.

If in the case of serious trouble the disco has to be stopped and the club closed early, make sure that young people have adequate means of getting home. When starting do not be afraid to start small with the club opening only one night a week for the 14–21 age group. Another night for the 12–15 age group might be considered but at this age boys are often disco-shy. A work evening should be arranged for repairs and refurbishing and perhaps Sunday afternoon meetings for discussion.

When the club is well attended there is money to pay the bills and part-time secretarial help; direction and other help has to be voluntary which fits in with the caring, Christian nature of the work. If there is one basic ingredient for this work it is love. Love and concern for young people and their families; love that will sponsor caring clubs like Parrot and Palm and the Parrot and Palm Development Agency which propagates new alcohol-free clubs and centres. Enthusiasm will often contribute cash to a new venture but it takes love to go on sponsoring, providing, strengthening, and encouraging in the years after the honeymoon enthusiasm for the new club is over.

Tim Mason has now left Worthing to become Diocesan Youth Officer in Swindon – a sad loss. But the work goes on at the Parrot and Palm Clubs in Worthing, Ealing, and Horsham which are the popular, practical pattern of the young person's alternative to the pub.

Alcohol and work

Introduction

It is now, at last, widely understood by those whose task it is to prevent or respond to alcohol-related problems that most problem drinkers are at work. Furthermore, for many excessive drinkers the work situation exacerbates the problem. The resultant costs to problem drinkers themselves, to fellow workers, and to employers in terms of sickness, absenteeism, reduced efficiency, accidents, and deteriorating relationships are considerable. If the problem drinking remains undetected it may lead to dismissal. For the employer, this means disruption to the workplace team and the expense of finding and training a replacement, which in some organizations may be substantial. For the dismissed employee, it means damage to self-respect, re-employment prospects, family relationships, and the chances of rehabilitation and recovery.

In 1981, *The Problem Drinker at Work*, a report by the Health and Safety Executive (HSE), the health departments, and the Department of Employment, (Health and Safety Executive, 1981) urged management and unions to develop alcohol and work policies. *The Problem Drinker at Work* picked up the point made earlier in the DHSS Advisory Committee on Alcoholism's report on *Prevention* (DHSS, 1978) that: 'both sides of industry should be pressed to recognize that this is not a problem which can be left to the health and personal social services. They too have responsibilities; they also stand to gain from a reduction in the incidence of alcohol-related impairment among personnel.'

The HSE's initiative prompted the Civil Service management and staff sides to begin negotiations over alcohol and work policies through the Whitley Council machinery. Several government departments have now adopted, or are in the process of adopting, their own policies. The Trades Union Congress (TUC) subsequently surveyed existing practices and issued its own guidelines on work-place policies, urging management and unions to work together to tackle alcohol abuse (TUC, 1976). One of the difficulties of trade unions and employers working together on the alcohol and work issue is that neither side is very well educated about what is involved. This is what makes the account by Robin Bunton and Roy Youdale of a trade union education project in Bristol so interesting. It reveals the unhelpful attitudes held by many trade unionists and suggests how these can gradually be overcome through active education and placing the issue of alcohol and work firmly in the context of health and safety rather than as a fringe matter outside the realms of 'real' collective bargaining.

But despite the TUC guidelines and the HSE advice most employers and trades unionists still tend to believe that the only 'alcohol problem' they are likely to encounter at work is the very occasional, stereotypical 'alcoholic'. Yet epidemiological evidence suggests that approximately 5 per cent of men and 1 per cent of women of working age can be expected to have some sort of drink problem (Wilson, 1980). As a result, alcohol-related accidents, absenteeism, sickness, and poor work performance contribute to the social cost to industry, conservatively estimated at £2,000 million annually (Maynard *et al.*, 1987)

Alcohol and work policies in the UK are no longer rare, particularly in the brewing and transport sectors and in organizations such as the Post Office, Marks and Spencer plc, a substantial minority of health authorities, and a handful of local government authorities. In the light of much of this work in major national private and public organizations a number of useful packages of materials have been produced. These include the industrial pack from the Institute of Alcohol Studies, 12 Caxton Street, London, SW1H 0QS, the Work Place Advisory Service pack from Alcohol Concern, 305 Gray's Inn Road, London, WC1X 8QF and Problem Drinking and the Workplace: a training pack from the Academic Department of Community Medicine, King's College Hospital, Denmark Hill, London, SE5.

In outline, an alcohol and work policy is simple. It is a statement, agreed by employer and workers' organizations, that a drinking problem is a health problem. It assures employees that those who are identified as having a problem or who themselves come forward for help will not endanger their jobs or their employment rights. It undertakes to assist towards appropriate aid and support. An alcohol and work policy is a statement of good intent. However, the success of a policy depends on how well it is implemented. Richard Cyster's account of his work with the Post Office shows very clearly how much work needs to be done in preparation for mounting even the most rudimentary educational programme. It emphasizes, as do many other chapters in this section on alcohol and work, the importance of ensuring the active involvement of participants. Cyster draws particular attention to the usefulness of addressing alcohol and work issues under a physical fitness rather than a purely health and illness heading. In an organization in which people are expected to be and consider themselves to be healthy this may well be the most appropriate kind of approach.

Any well-rounded alcohol and work policy is made up of three components: case identification, education, and good practice. The programme will have a 'case identification' component since the mere existence of a policy will not automatically lead to problem drinkers in a workforce coming forward for help. There will be an 'education' component to inform the workforce about the difficulties that excessive drinking can cause, about the industrial hazards of alcohol misuse, and about the help that is available for those who need it.

The 'good practices' component will reflect the organization's overall attitude towards alcohol and will be embodied in the day-to-day activities of each workplace department, trade, or profession. In all three of its aspects a properly operational alcohol and work policy is everybody's business within a place of employment. But as with most specific problems it does, in practice, help enormously to have the responsibility for pushing forward activities and innovations squarely on somebody's desk. Richard Quail's account of the establishment of a special unit within London Regional Transport to give support to the whole alcohol and work enterprise is very instructive. The unit is a focal point both within the organization to review cases and give guidance to action and also for those outside the organization as a point of liaison with treatment agencies over referral criteria and treatment regimes.

Local prevention workers, as is stressed throughout this book, have to press for prevention. In relation to alcohol and work issues this means seizing every local opportunity for making public statements about alcohol and work policies and stressing their value in an overall pattern and range of local activities. The opportunity for such public statements may be provided by discussion on alcohol and health and safety issues in the local media, or created by a deliberate decision to discuss alcohol and work in local branch meetings of professional organizations or groups. Local prevention workers must know which local organizations have policies, what those policies contain, and the impact of those policies in terms of changes in behaviour, levels of knowledge about alcohol issues, problems identified, and people helped.

The importance of local knowledge cannot be over-emphasized. This is brought home very vividly in Audrey Harvey's account of her work with the Aberdeen stevedores which clearly shows that policy and practice does not develop in a vacuum. It was essential for her to understand the local drinking and occupational culture before even beginning to introduce any alcohol and work education programme. Her case study is also useful in that it reminds us that out there in the real world we cannot expect organizations and groups to 'play by all the accepted rules'. As she points out there was no 'confidentiality' on the docks about intimate personal problems. That does tend to undermine the cook-book approach to handling problems. As those who have been heavily involved in alcohol education generally and alcohol and work education in particular know only too well, it is almost always necessary to start from scratch in any particular organization. So although national guidance and exhortation and ready-made training packs are very useful they can only be supplementary to the hard work which has to go on at the local level.

Every locality has a complex network of groups with a direct interest in health and safety at work issues. They should be contacted by local prevention workers and supported in their task of promoting alcohol and work policies. The network is likely to include, for example, the Area Office of the HSE which is closely linked with the Employment Medical Advisory Service (EMAS), which itself provides information and advice on health and safety at work to the HSE and to employees. The local Environmental Health Department (EHD) will have access to a wide range of local workplaces. The developing health education function within EHDs provides them with an important opportunity for promoting alcohol and work policies. Coroners, all of whom have to deal with industrial fatalities, should be acquainted with the concept of alcohol and work policies and the content of sensible policies. They have the right to comment on matters which require attention to prevent further deaths and any reference by a coroner to the desirability of alcohol and work policies would stimulate local debate.

Giving publicity to the need for alcohol and work policies and encouraging local groups of key workers to develop an interest in the issue is essential. However, there are more direct opportunities for specific local prevention workers to promote alcohol and work policies. It is inconsistent, for example, for health professionals to urge others to adopt well-designed policies if their own workplaces do not have policies or if those policies are poorly constructed. Some district health authorities have alcohol and work policies but many do not. Moreover some authorities could certainly improve what are clearly 'paper policies'.

Building support within the workplace for a policy may take time. But, at a minimum, occupational health nurses and others could urge the adoption of some of the 'good practices' which were outlined in *Preventing Alcohol Problems: A Guide to Local Action* (Tether and Robinson, 1986). Specific good practices can be introduced without a fully fledged alcohol and work policy. Indeed it may be sensible in many workplaces to encourage a policy to evolve out of an accumulation of good practices rather than to construct a policy and expect good practices to follow automatically. The importance of starting in a small way and building up towards formal policies is illustrated in Ken Painter's description of a 'soft' approach to industry. His piece is particularly useful in that it emphasizes, again, that life at the local level is not easy. Doing any kind of alcohol and work promotion requires dedication, hard work, and a great deal of time. Producing policies at head office is easy. Implementing them out in the branches is jolly difficult.

Alcohol and work policies should be visible and well-publicized components of every locality's prevention strategy. The advocacy and participation of local prevention workers is vital if good policies are to be promoted and some of the health, social, and financial costs associated with alcohol misuse are to be reduced.

References

Department of Health and Social Security, Advisory Committee on Alcoholism (1978) *Prevention*, London: DHSS.

Health and Safety Executive (1981) *The Problem Drinker at Work*, the health departments and the Department of Employment, London: HMSO.

Maynard, A., Hardman, G., and Whelan, A. (1987) 'Measuring the Social Costs of Addictive Substances', *British Journal of Addiction* 82, 6: 701–6.

Tether, P. and Robinson, D. (1986) *Preventing Alcohol Problems: A Guide to Local Action*, London: Tavistock.

Trades Union Congress (1976) *Safety and Health at Work*, London: TUC.

Wilson, P. (1980) *Drinking in England and Wales*, a Survey by the Office of Population Censuses and Surveys for the DHSS, London: HMSO.

A trade union education project

Robin Bunton and Roy Youdale

In the spring of 1985 at the offices of the Avon Council on Alcoholism (ACA) in Bristol, we met with David Gover, the South-West Regional Education Officer for the TUC, to plan the first of what was to become a series of one-day courses on alcohol and work for local trade union representatives and full-time officials.

A couple of months before that meeting, an outreach worker at the ACA, who had been researching the information and education needs of various local groups in relation to alcohol, had contacted Phil Gregory, the Secretary of the South-West TUC, who had acknowledged that alcohol at work was an important issue for trade unionists but one which had as yet been given little detailed thought by most unions. After a brief discussion, it was agreed that the best way to raise the issue initially was to organize a pilot one-day course or 'workshop' at a local Trade Union Studies Centre. This would be under the auspices of the TUC Regional Education Service, but very much in conjunction with the ACA.

Over a series of three meetings the details of the aims, structure, teaching methods, and materials were worked out and the first workshop was held in June 1985. Since then a further three workshops have been held – in December 1985, in November 1986, and in March 1987. The one-day course is now offered each year as part of the TUC Regional Education programme.

How the workshops were organized

It was agreed from the start that the workshops should be offered as part of the TUC regional programme of courses for trade unionists, which are for the most part organized during working time. Union representatives have a legal right under the Employment Protection (Consolidation) Act 1978 to paid time off from work to attend TUC or union approved courses on topics relating to 'collective bargaining and industrial relations duties'. However, this right is qualified by the need for union representatives to negotiate with employers over the direct relevance of the courses and over when and how much time off is to be taken. This was one of the first hurdles for the workshops to overcome.

Many employers still see the problem of alcohol and work as a straightforward disciplinary matter and not as a topic for negotiation or collective bargaining, and so not eligible for paid educational release. Relatively low numbers attended the workshops (between seven and twelve), and some of the workshops were cancelled due to insufficient recruitment. This was almost certainly a reflection of reluctance by employers to release union representatives rather than of a lack of concern about the issue on the part of the reps themselves.

TUC courses for trade unionists are developed and overseen by the TUC Education Department nationally and regionally. But they are actually taught by tutors at local authority colleges and polytechnics and by tutors from the Workers' Education Association. The broad educational philosophy of TUC courses can be likened to an old Chinese proverb: 'I hear and forget. I see and remember. I do and understand.' In other words the emphasis is very much on students 'doing' and participating through discussion, rather than sitting back and being lectured at. It is important to appreciate this educational perspective in order to understand the eventual content of the workshop. The other key element in TUC educational thinking is the absence of any idea that education is neutral or value-free. On the contrary, trade union education makes a point of stating the assumptions on which it is based and the point of view which it is trying to argue in relation to any given topic.

The starting point of the course planning was the question: in what ways does alcohol at work pose a problem for trade union reps? For our initial discussion it was clear that there were a number of key issues:

- The lack of knowledge by union reps and their members and by employers and managers of how alcohol affects the body and behaviour;
- the unhelpful attitudes towards the problem expressed at times by all the above groups;
- the difficulty of deciding when someone at work has 'a drink problem', and how to assess how many alcohol-related problems there are at a given workplace;
- the problem of how to approach and help someone with a known or suspected drink problem, and where to get help and advice;
- the concern with how to defend members threatened with disciplinary action for alcohol-related problems;
- the question of how to raise alcohol-related problems as a negotiating/collective bargaining issue with employers.

On the basis of this rather formidable list, we then had to decide what basic approach the course was going to take. To an extent this was straightforward since the TUC already had a draft policy on alcohol and work. This was in line with the views of the ACA in that alcohol-related problems should be viewed as a matter of health and illness and not simply regarded as a disciplinary issue.

We now had enough to set out a series of three clear aims for the workshop, which would be printed on the course publicity material. These aims were to help union reps:

to understand the effects of alcohol on behaviour and the implications of this for trade union members at work;
to assess the extent of alcohol-related problems at their workplace, and
to devise a trade union strategy for dealing with such problems, which sees alcohol dependence as a treatable *illness* and not simply as a disciplinary issue.

The programme for the day emerged as:

Morning	*Afternoon*
1 Introduction and course aims 2 The facts about alcohol (video and questionnaire activity) 3 Identifying alcohol-related problems at work 4 Taking up alcohol-related problems	5 Developing a trade union strategy for dealing with alcohol-related problems at work: – employers' policies (alcohol and health and safety) – procedures – education for members – sources of advice and information 6 Course review

Note: Sessions 3, 4, and 5 were run as small group (3 or 4 people) activities, each followed by a discussion involving the whole course.

We also agreed that it was important to have two tutors working as a team to run the workshop – one to provide specific expertise in relation to alcohol problems and the other to provide the basic trade union studies framework.

Problems and successes

Dealing with an emotive issue such as alcohol in an educational context is not easy. One of the problems we faced right from the start was the familiar attitude openly expressed or implied by the union reps that alcohol is really only a problem for a few people who go 'over the top', and that all that is needed is a more sympathetic way of dealing with them. It was difficult to get the reps to move to a position where they could see alcohol as a potential problem for anyone, and could consider, for example, examining their own drinking habits.

There was also the problem of some union reps, for example from British Rail and the NHS, taking the view that disciplinary action was entirely appropriate for members who put other people at serious risk of accidents through their use of alcohol. As tutors, we tried to argue, not always successfully, that disciplinary action should be a last resort, and that several other steps could be taken before it was invoked.

Many reps were pessimistic about the possibility of bringing the issue of alcohol into the arena of collective bargaining, because of what they saw as intransigent attitudes of their managements and, in many cases, of their own members. Most reps had come to the workshops because a colleague at work or a relative had an alcohol problem. One of the key things they wanted from the course, which we were not really able to give them, was the 'answer' to the problem of how to tell when someone 'has a drink problem', how to approach and help someone they know or suspect has a problem, or how to defend union members facing disciplinary action by management for alcohol-related problems.

On the *plus* side, the general feeling at the end of each workshop was that it had been useful and two common themes ran through the course reviews:

> that the information given out – on the basic facts about alcohol and its effects; on alcohol policies for employers; and on sources of help and advice – was very helpful and gave people a new perspective on alcohol;
>
> that the information and course discussion had given the reps the confidence to raise the issue of alcohol back at their own workplace – whether in a fairly low key way by asking for simple factual literature to be distributed to everyone or at a more ambitious level by trying to renegotiate a disciplinary procedure or a full alcohol policy.

Two tangible examples of 'success' in relation to the workshops can also be cited. A senior union rep from the Confederation of Health Service Employees (COHSE), who came to the first workshop in June 1985, has been the driving force behind the development within his district health authority in Bristol of an alcohol policy for all staff, a process that began before the workshop took place and which is nearing completion after two years. A union rep from a large engineering employer in Bristol went back and did a small survey of drinking habits among some colleagues at work, using a drinking diary. As a moderate drinker himself, he was horrified to discover that of the dozen people he surveyed the lowest figure in units of alcohol consumed in the previous week was 70 (i.e. 35 pints of beer or the equivalent) and the highest 110 (55 pints). He said that this had led him to cut down the amount he drank.

It must be stressed, however, that it is still too early to assess the practical effect of the workshops since the process of developing awareness about alcohol and work is a slow and uneven one. It should also be said that trade unions are only one, albeit very important, group that is able to contribute to that process. Personnel managers and employers, voluntary agencies, and individual workers themselves can all make a valuable contribution to bringing about effective change.

Conclusion

In 1986 the Labour Research Department reported that only 27 per cent of the employers they surveyed had a formal policy. These were mainly in the public sector, e.g. British Rail, the Post Office, the Civil Service, the NHS, and the recently privatized British Telecom. Even where such policies exist, they are not always supported by effective training programmes – particularly for junior line managers – and trade unions are often not fully involved in the design and implementation of the policy. There is still a long way to go.

In terms of trade union education about alcohol and work, some of the key lessons to emerge from the workshops so far are that:

- much of the course discussion is almost bound to centre around people's attitudes to alcohol and its misuse, and it is very important to try and locate this discussion in a collective rather than just an individual context. This is difficult and delicate work which can easily go wrong, but plenty of time should be allowed for it;
- it is important for union reps on the course to be able to take away a fair amount of useful practical information. They should not be overwhelmed by having to try to absorb it all on the course itself;
- in terms of bargaining for paid release to attend courses, the issue of alcohol and work should be placed firmly in the context of health and safety at work, rather than seen as a fringe issue outside the realms of 'real' collective bargaining.

Where do we go from here? We would like to try running a pilot two-day workshop for union reps in which the issue of alcohol would be placed in the wider context of a whole range of drugs, from caffeine to cocaine. We envisage, however, that the issue of alcohol would still occupy at least half the time on the course.

Note

For a copy of the basic material and activities used on the workshops, please write to: David Gover, South-West TUC Regional Education Officer, 1 Henbury Road, Westbury-on-Trym, Bristol, BS9 3HH.

Useful materials

Problem Drinking: TUC guidelines for a workplace policy, TUC, Congress House, Great Russell Street, London WC1B 3LS, December 1986, 80p.

The Problem Drinker at Work, Health and Safety Executive, HMSO, 1981, £1.50.

'Alcohol Policies: calling time on problem drinking', from *Bargaining Report*, December 1986, Labour Research Department, 78 Blackfriars Road, London SE1 8HF.

Workplace Advisory Service Information Pack, Alcohol Concern, 305 Gray's Inn Road, London WC1X 8QF (Tel: 01 833 3471), 1986, £4.00.

'Alcohol and Drugs: Programmes of Assistance for Workers', *Conditions of Work Digest*, vol. 6, no. 1, 1987, ILO Publications, International Labour Office, CH-1211 Geneva 22, Switzerland, £14.55.

Someone Like You, Post Office training video (19 minutes), 1986, available from: Luke Lockyer, 33 Grosvenor Place, London (Tel: 01 245 7540); or Academic Department of Community Medicine, King's College Hospital, Denmark Hill, London.

Problem Drinking and the Workplace: a seminar on the management of alcohol problems in employment (training pack), Academic Department of Community Medicine, King's College School of Medicine and Dentistry and the Health Education Council, 78 Oxford Street, London, 1987.

Alcohol education at the workplace: a co-operative venture

Richard Cyster

This article describes a co-operative venture by the Post Office and the Health Education Authority (HEA) – then the Health Education Council. The Post Office, although having no more serious an alcohol problem than other employers, had taken the decision to introduce a policy on problem drinking at work. The policy contained a substantial health education and training remit, and the HEA were interested in the possibilities of the workplace as a context for health education in general and alcohol education in particular. The project was based at King's College School of Medicine and Dentistry and began in December 1983. Its aim was to develop, implement, and evaluate materials for use in alcohol education and training at the workplace, with the Post Office acting as a 'testbed'. There were two sets of materials:

- training materials for use with those responsible for operating the Post Office problem drinking policy;
- education materials for use with the whole workforce at a more general level, providing information on the nature and effects of alcohol and the problems arising from its misuse.

A fuller description of the methods and findings of the project can be found elsewhere (Cyster and McEwen, 1986a). What follows here is an account of the approaches undertaken, the difficulties encountered, and some of the lessons that were learned.

Training

Support for the project at Post Office Headquarters was assured but similar co-operation at local level had still to be sought and achieved. It was, of course, at the local level that the project was actually to be conducted. Visits to a number of Post Office regions and discussions with management, occupational health and welfare staff, and trade union representatives helped to clarify both the nature and the extent of the alcohol problems currently being experienced. The visits also provided an indication of the style and content of the training that was required. These discussions provided a basis for the design of the first two training seminars conducted with representatives from the Post Office Occupational Health Service and Welfare Departments. Each was attended by twenty-five participants drawn from all regions of the UK. The purpose of these seminars was to prepare those who would serve as first point of referral for employees with suspected drinking problems, to provide information on how the existence of a problem might be identified, and to assess the initial counselling required. The seminars also served as a pilot for future seminars with management and unions.

Further discussions with representatives at the Post Office's North-West region secured their willingness to serve as a trial area for the management/union seminars. Governing the organization and conduct of the seminars was the decision to involve Occupational Health and Welfare staff directly in their presentation. There were two reasons for this:

> OH and Welfare staff, already familiar with the Post Office regional organization, would be able to relate information and training provided by the seminar to pre-existing structures and procedures within the workplace; those members of the OHS and Welfare staff involved in the seminar would eventually be able to take over from the Project Officer and run further seminars on their own behalf.

It was also decided that both management and trades union representatives should be invited to attend each seminar. If unions and management had the opportunity to discuss together how best to identify and deal with drinking problems, then all parties could benefit, not least by avoiding the internecine strife which often occurs in these situations.

Unfortunately, shortly before the first of the seminars, the Project Officer was involved in a serious road accident. I was in hospital for two months and the seminar was too near to allow for postponement or cancellation. It proceeded according to the initial plan, with some help from an outside agency and using materials already prepared by the project. The positive reactions from participants persuaded the OH and Welfare staff of their own abilities as seminar presenters. It also helped to overcome a problem all too common in development projects such as this – the over-dependence on the Project Officer as the perceived 'expert'. I would hesitate, however, to recommend such a drastic solution to other projects faced with a similar difficulty! But on my return to work I found myself working as part of a team rather than carrying the sole responsibilities for the presentation of future seminars.

Seminar objectives and evaluation

Following discussions with local Post Office staff, it was agreed that the objectives of the seminars were:

- to educate the audience on the nature and effects of alcohol, on the widespread problems arising from its abuse, and on the prevalence of alcohol-related problems at the workplace;
- to make the audience aware that alcohol problems occur at the Post Office and to discuss methods of identifying and coping with them within the laid-down Post Office policy and procedures;
- to identify and agree an 'Action Plan' to counter the incidence of alcohol abuse at the Post Office.

Six seminars were held in the Post Office's North-Western and Scottish regions, each organized with full local co-operation and support. Each seminar was made up of sessions which covered the following topics:

Alcohol, the individual, and society
Alcohol and work
Post Office policy and procedure
Identifying problem drinkers
Referral and denial
Guidance, help, and follow-up
Group discussions
Action plans

Use was also made of a film on the American postal service's 'Program for Alcoholic Recovery'. Unfortunately, seminar participants occasionally found the US situation too far from their own experience to draw any useful lessons.

Evaluation of the seminar materials was achieved by questionnaire survey of participants immediately following the seminar and by a further questionnaire and discussion at a follow-up meeting about two months later. This allowed for continuing adjustment of the seminar design and content according to participants' reactions. The results of the evaluation suggest that participants considered the seminars to have been successful in educating about the nature and effects of alcohol; raising awareness of the prevalence of alcohol problems in the workplace; and providing a basis for discussion of suitable methods for dealing with such problems. And *less* effective in providing guidance on the identification and referral of problem drinkers.

These reactions have informed the design and content of the training pack produced by the project: *Problem Drinking and the Workplace: A Seminar on the Management of Alcohol Problems in Employment* (Cyster and McEwen, 1986b). Adopting a modular approach, adjustable to a variety of occupational settings, it lays emphasis on audience participation, guided discussion, and practical approaches to dealing with alcohol problems at work. It includes a section designed to accompany the training video which was produced by the Post Office, entitled *Someone Like You.*

Workforce education

The Post Office employs over 180,000 staff distributed throughout the UK. It was clearly impossible to evaluate educational materials aimed at the workforce en masse, so a sample of 4,000 staff was identified, based at one sorting office in Central London. Consistent with the provisions of the policy on problem drinking, the objectives of the health education materials were:

to increase knowledge of the nature and effects of alcohol and alcohol problems;
to publicize the Post Office policy on problem drinking among employees;
to promote positive attitudes to sensible drinking.

As with the training initiatives, the first requirement was to secure management and union support at the local office. Management's support was achieved without difficulty but although clearance for the project had already been negotiated with the Post Office unions at national level, I encountered enormous suspicion about its aims and methods from the union representatives based at the local level. I had great difficulty in convincing them I was not a management 'hatchet man' and that the project was not intended to identify problem drinkers for dismissal. A residual suspicion may have contributed to the difficulties which were experienced later.

The form and content of the educational materials developed for local trial were agreed following discussion with local OHS representatives and influenced by the results of a preliminary survey of the target population. It was decided to develop a computer quiz along the lines of those already in use with the OHS Roadshow (see page 92) to provide information on alcohol and its effects; and to make a short five-minute video about the nature and effect of alcohol for showing to invited audiences. This was to serve as a trigger for discussion rather than as a 'stand alone' initiative. Both would attempt to provide information on alcohol and on the problems arising from its abuse in an interesting, non-censorious manner. In addition, I advised the OHS on the development of a booklet entitled *The Good Booze Guide* which was issued to all Post Office staff during December 1984.

The quiz and video were piloted with staff at the local London office in October 1985. Both were well received by those actually taking part. The before-and-after questionnaire surveys revealed a significant increase in knowledge about the nature and effects of alcohol among participants compared with non-participants. No change in attitudes to alcohol was revealed. The main difficulty faced by both initiatives was the relatively low level of participation by the target audience, with approximately 100 trying the quiz and 600 seeing the video – even though the latter was shown in working time. This reluctance may have been due to the perceived irrelevance of what was on offer. It may also have been due to the residual suspicion which was mentioned earlier, a suspicion fed by a series of unfortunately worded posters displayed around the office at that time. This was part of a unilateral drive by local management against what they saw as the growing disciplinary problems resulting from alcohol misuse.

The OHS Roadshow

A more productive approach to the issue of alcohol and work was offered by the inclusion of alcohol as one subject in a broader-based health education initiative.

Launched in January 1985, the Post Office's 'OHS Roadshow' consisted of a mobile health education exhibition covering smoking, alcohol, and diet. It visited head post offices and regional headquarters throughout the UK. In addition to the exhibition panels, the Roadshow included tests for height, weight, blood pressure, and lung function, as well as a computer-based quiz on diet and heart disease, and a lifestyle analysis. Advice was available from the OHS staff on diet, stopping smoking, and reducing blood pressure.

Observations of three Roadshow events suggested that the most popular sections were the interactive ones, especially those on the computer. Staff queued to have their lung function checked or to try the lifestyle analysis. Sections of the Roadshow that did not feature a participatory element attracted few visitors. To increase the participatory element in the alcohol component of the Roadshow, it was decided to include the computer alcohol quiz at future events. The quiz consists of ten questions on the nature and effects of alcohol and takes 5–10 minutes to complete. For each question the user is given two opportunities of selecting the correct answer from the three options supplied. The computer itself then gives the correct answer together with some additional information. At the end of the quiz the user is given a score out of ten.

Evaluation by means of a before-and-after questionnaire survey of the target audience at one office visited by the Roadshow showed it to be equally as effective as alcohol education alone in raising knowledge about alcohol. More importantly, the Roadshow was seen by over 40 per cent of the target audience and a similar level of penetration was achieved at other offices visited. But perhaps the most significant finding of the evaluation exercise was that half the respondents who visited the Roadshow had done so to see how fit they were. They saw their visit in positive terms as a chance to learn about their present health status and about ways to improve it. Learning about alcohol was just part of this wider approach.

Summing up

Experience gained from this project has underlined the importance of a co-operative approach to health education at the workplace. Alcohol education and indeed the wider process of implementing an alcohol policy is not something done *to* and *for* industry, but *with* it. Extensive consultation with representatives of all sections of the organization (medical, welfare, management, union, etc.) helps to ensure that content and delivery are appropriate to local needs and conditions. Involvement of local OHS, medical, and welfare staff contributes to the continuation of any training initiatives once the initial stimulus is removed.

A major difficulty with alcohol education, of course, is that those people for whom drinking presents no problem may see it as irrelevant, while those who do experience problems are lothe to admit to them. This difficulty may be compounded at the workplace by employees' suspicions that health education on alcohol represents just more management 'interference' with spare time activities. So, any approach to alcohol education at work must be participative and non-censorious. My experience with the Post Office project also suggests that the inclusion of alcohol within a broader health education and fitness approach may go some way to circumventing the problems of 'irrelevance' and management 'interference' outlined above.

As a result of support from the Health Education Authority, the Post Office, and Shell UK, the project was extended for a second phase, beginning in April 1986. The materials are being further developed and refined in continued co-operation with the Post Office and in a new association with Shell UK.

References

Cyster, R. and McEwen, J. (1986a) *Alcohol Education at the Workplace*, Final Report to the Health Education Council.

Cyster, R. and McEwen, J. (1986b) *Problem Drinking and the Workplace: A Seminar on the Management of Alcohol Problems in Employment*, London: Health Education Council. (Copies are available from the authors at the Department of Community Medicine, King's College School of Medicine and Dentistry, Denmark Hill, London SE5 8RX.)

Acknowledgement

This article is based on a research project funded by the Health Education Authority and conducted with the active help and co-operation of the Post Office, both of whom the author gratefully acknowledges.

Alcohol and work performance: the role of a special unit

Richard G. Quail

London Regional Transport (LRT) is responsible for the provision of passenger transport services in the Greater London area. It is descended from the London Passenger Transport Board which was established in 1933. LRT currently employs approximately 48,000 staff in London Underground and London Buses – the two main businesses responsible for operating services – subsidiary concerns, and central support services such as catering, health, and welfare. In addition to obvious occupations, such as bus and train drivers, the organization employs a variety of trades and professions and negotiates with several different unions and staff associations. LRT has a world-wide reputation for its performance as a transport company and has an international subsidiary employing transport consultants whose expertise is sought in a variety of countries. It is perhaps then hardly surprising that it should have taken an initiative in the area of the effects of alcohol on work performance.

In terms of alcohol-related problems, there are reasons to believe that LRT has less than the average incidence amongst its workforce. Two specific factors are significant:

- The rules and regulations governing public service vehicle licensing demand high standards of health and fitness from the licence holders. Medical examination requirements exist for many of the company's staff which would not normally occur in most other occupations. Alcohol problems can consequently be detected during these routine compulsory health checks, and indeed, potential risks can be spotted, and eliminated, at the recruitment medical stage.
- Many of the company's staff are in clear view of and in contact with the public for long periods of the working day. Their performance, therefore, is the subject of constant scrutiny. It is not easy for many of these staff to hide their behaviour or appearance from view as might be the case in jobs having a lower public profile.

The organization was fortunate to have, already established, a comprehensive medical service, a network of personnel officers, and an Industrial Welfare

Service. The combined experience of these specialists was used to discuss, and eventually produce a corporate statement outlining the company attitude to the use and abuse of alcohol and other drugs. This statement of policy further described the constructive help available to any employee considering him or herself to have a problem. The statement was certainly not proffered as a 'soft option' and did not preclude disciplinary action where appropriate. It did, however, provide for the fair and proper management of alcohol-related problems, with the emphasis on prevention, both of the initial difficulties associated with substance abuse and of recurrence in such instances as problems were detected.

Making a statement concerning alcohol misuse in itself was not a particularly unusual step for a British company to take. Resourcing a specialist unit to co-ordinate the non-medical aspects of such a statement appeared to be somewhat more adventurous. London Regional Transport was rightly satisfied that its medical office was providing the necessary support and expertise to deal with medical contingencies. There are, however, many aspects of alcohol misuse whose problem potential is essentially social and whose detection and solution demand the skills of different disciplines.

Initial action involved listing the components required to support a response towards alcohol in the workplace and decide which of these could and should be provided by the company and which should properly be provided by outside resources.

Three key ingredients eventually emerged, which in chronological sequence are: education, support to management, and referral.

Education

This is needed on two levels, concerning, first, the existence of the policy statement, the responsibilities of management and staff under the terms of the statement, and the details of the support service – how, where, when, and why to use it. And second, the recognition of alcohol problems in the work place.

Practice experience had shown that these factors could be treated separately without damaging their prospects for being effective. In many cases education about the policy statement and the support service was a useful preliminary to the effort to educate about factors of recognition.

Information regarding the support service could be communicated to the businesses in a short precise session – often included in a general meeting agenda. This gave management the opportunity to publicise the service in advance of finding the time to arrange the more comprehensive and time-consuming recognition training.

Support to management

GPs, hospitals, the police, the courts, the probation service, and social workers have for many years displayed an ambivalent attitude towards people presenting alcohol problems. All too often the attitude has been to ignore the problem and hope that it goes away. If this is the attitude of the professionals responsible specifically for handling this type of situation, how realistic is it to expect line management in a transport industry from amongst their many and varied tasks to give any sort of priority to these problems? To help those lacking specific knowledge or experience to deal with individual problem cases, the LRT Welfare Office established a permanent, full-time consultancy available to all LRT management. The consultancy was established as the Alcohol Education Unit in 1984 and provides two specific services.

First, when an employee-related problem occurs the Unit offers reasonable confirmation should there be any area of doubt that it is, in fact, a case involving alcohol misuse. This is done by a close examination of the generally accepted performance-related indicators and assessment of the various oral and written information available. Following confirmation, the situation is then discussed with the manager with regard to any necessary action. In many instances the actual nature of the job being done may well be a contributory factor to the maintenance of the problem. If, for example, the individual works in considerable isolation a move to a more supervised environment would almost certainly be recommended.

Second, the Unit undertakes to interview the individual with a view to assessing the nature and extent of the alcohol involvement in order that a course of treatment or other action can be recommended. This once again relies on the generally accepted patterns of deterioration in order to ascertain the degree of any social and potential medical degeneration being experienced. In all instances this information is fed back to the individual along with any recommendation for action.

In cases referred as the result of disciplinary action, information regarding the extent of any damage plus any recommended response is also given to the management. Detailed personal information remains confidential between the individual and the Unit. It has been shown by experience that in order for full advantage to be taken of this service, it is necessary for the Alcohol Unit's staff to be prepared to travel to interviews with management and employees. The potential for success would almost certainly diminish considerably if management, especially, were expected to find the time to attend the Unit. The other demands on their time plus the complexity of most cases would almost certainly discourage management from taking action. Simply, to be effective the Unit's service must be freely available. Bearing this fact in mind and the 24-hour service offered by LRT, consultations at one o'clock in the morning are, if infrequent, not unheard of.

Referral

In the past, referral into treatment had tended to be something of a hit and miss affair. Where an individual ended up depended on who was responsible for the intervention and the extent of their experience or knowledge of handling alcohol-related problems. If the situation was handled by the local manager or personnel staff then it might have been Alcoholics Anonymous or the Local Council on Alcoholism who were involved. In many cases the individual would have been expected to fit the known potential for treatment rather than the treatment being selected in the light of its appropriateness. Whilst it is recognized that in certain areas the options for intervention are somewhat limited, it does not seem desirable to leave this crucial area open to such a pot-luck approach.

The other side of this equation relates to the need for the treatment agencies to be aware of the attitude and potential for support of any employer who might provide them with clients. All too often any contact between company and agency is made around the urgency of a specific crisis where the need to respond to a particular individual overrides the 'less pressing' need to establish the ground rules. The criteria for obtaining assistance from the agency, the co-operation needed from the employer, and the degree and nature of information to be passed between the agency and the organization should ideally be established prior to the actual referral of any potential client. If these areas are fully discussed before being used then, it is hoped, any embarrassing misunderstanding can be avoided. Generally speaking the only information required by the employer is whether or not an individual has made contact – is he or she being invited into continuing treatment and, should it terminate, is this by mutual agreement or is it the result of an initiative taken by either party?

The value of any intervention with regard to work performance is best assessed by the employer. The employer will also need to know something of the requirements of the treatment regime especially if a period of, for example, day attendance is required which would necessitate absence from work. As a passenger transport organization LRT has statutory and moral responsibilities to ensure the safety of passengers and colleagues of an employee who is undergoing treatment. Where safety conditions are involved, therefore, it may be necessary for the employer to arrange alternative duties or, in some circumstances, to negotiate a period of sickness absence.

The Alcohol Education Unit of LRT has spent a considerable amount of time getting to know the treatment agencies in and around Greater London. The agencies have been approached concerning their referral criteria and treatment regimes whilst being offered in return a description of the service available within LRT, its aim, objectives, and responsibilities.

Methods of contact have been established and the nature and extent of continuous contact agreed. It has been found that without exception the agencies have welcomed the opportunity to establish a good working practice prior to any referral, and the practices that have been established have shown themselves to be easily usable and adequate for all intended purposes.

In short, this pre-emptive approach gives two distinct advantages to the company:

- it has established the level and nature of feedback available to any manager prior to considering any action;
- it has allowed the Unit, during the client assessment, to attempt to refer the client to the most appropriate treatment resource rather than simply to the agency which first comes to mind.

In order for this 'referral' aspect to function properly, it has become necessary to channel all the information from the various agencies, and on various clients, through one co-ordinating clearing house; thus ensuring a standardization of approach in all instances.

A further advantage of considered and co-ordinated referral is that it allows for early contact with LRT's own medical service with regard to fitness for duty and advice concerning any individual employee's physical well-being. This works both ways – where they feel it appropriate the medical department refer members of staff to the Alcohol Unit.

In those cases where significant and considerable non-medical intervention is required this is sought from outside specialists. It is felt that there are several competent and experienced agencies within the potential catchment area whose expertise and resources LRT could never match.

Conclusion

The Alcohol Education Unit represents one of a range of approaches adopted by LRT in order to best equip the Operating and Personnel Management to maintain high standards with regard to passenger and staff safety and sickness absence trends. Such an initiative reflects the longstanding concern for the proper control of all the factors which make up a public transport environment.

The Unit provides management with the ability to recognize and respond to potential and actual problems. It also plays its part in promoting the sensible use of alcohol. Emphasis has been continually placed on developing those techniques and skills already inherent within LRT in order that they might be adapted to manage the effects of alcohol misuse on work performance.

As an integral part of the structure, the Alcohol Education Unit has a good understanding of the LRT organization. It has gained from supportive internal working relationships and is considered to have established itself with some credit. The Unit offers a readily available resource which is sympathetic to the needs of the company and, therefore, able to provide an acceptable service to its staff.

On the docks: awareness sessions with stevedores

Audrey Harvey

When I said to people in 1986 that I was working in the dock area, meaningful looks were exchanged and ribald comments abounded. These reactions made me look at my own assumptions about harbour areas and dockers. Contacts with the Aberdeen Stevedoring Company management and men, and private visits at various hours of the day and night have considerably increased my knowledge of the docks, the environs, and the pubs. I hope I can convey to you the challenge, satisfaction, and fun I have experienced from the work so far and in the continuing pursuit of an acceptable policy to deal with alcohol-related problems.

How did I come to be involved? The Aberdeen Alcohol Advisory and Counselling Service (AACS) is committed to a wide range of initiatives, and a large part of my work as director is concerned with prevention. No better scene for such a focus exists than the workplace, and regular involvement with local radio and press has helped to heighten this awareness in the Grampian Region.

A director of the Aberdeen Stevedoring Company and the nursing sister employed by the National Dock Labour Board, who were both aware of drink problems across their whole workforce, approached AACS for advice on how other companies tackled alcohol problems. In order to offer specific advice, I then had to do my homework and find out about:

> Dock Labour Schemes and their effect on present-day thinking of the Aberdeen Stevedoring Company;
> who or what was the Aberdeen Stevedoring Company? What were the management/workforce relationships and the disciplinary measures?;
> what was the local drinking 'scene' and what were the attitudes to drinking in the dock area?

Only when this preliminary work was done could I begin to devise appropriate alcohol awareness events.

Dock labour schemes and the Aberdeen Stevedoring Company

No organized trade union existed in the dock industry until the 'Tanner strike' of 1889 – led by Ben Tillett – to get a wage rise from 5d to 6d per hour. The strike achieved its goal and the Dock Wharf and Riverside Labourers Union was formed in London. Other large ports followed until in 1907 there were 150,000 members in the UK. Stable conditions of employment were, however, non-existent. Various committees of enquiry addressed themselves nationally to the problem with no success until the outbreak of the Second World War, when, as a result of the efforts of Ernest Bevin, then Minister of Labour, various pieces of legislation were implemented to tackle the major problem of decasualization. These were:

1940 – Dock Labour (Compulsory Registration)
1942 – National Dock Labour Corporation Ltd formed
1943 – Dock Workers (Regulations of Employment) Act
1947 – Dock Workers (Regulations of Employment) Order

Guidelines for recruitment, training, welfare, allocation to employers and their responsibility for registering their cargoes and workforce requirements were imposed, so that a regular workforce was bonded by a common purpose and stable working conditions to achieve maximum potential.

After the Second World War unrest was again rife until, following the report of the Devlin Committee, a new Order of Employment was enacted in 1967. This brought together all the temporary war-time schemes and made them mandatory for all those handling significant cargo. Ports had to be registered and returns made to the government detailing allocation and performance of cargo handling and workers used. A levy was imposed on employers to defray the scheme. A minimum weekly wage was paid and training, holiday pay, pension rights, and employment protection ratified in line with other workforces. Local negotiations were, however, still viable.

On the Aberdeen docks at this time there were 168 general cargo workers and 42 coal workers. The latter – known as the Blue Badgers – were a lower grade of docker employed to discharge coal or other heavy manual and poorly paid cargoes. All men were registered with the National Dock Labour Board (NDLB) in an open pool situation. Each employer had a 'free call' and foremen would pick and choose at will. If dockers were not 'called' for work, the NDLB gave them a 'duck egg'. This meant that their work book was stamped – with an oval stamp – and they were entitled to nine shillings for that day, with a maximum of £4.9s. for a week. When the 1967 Devlin Order came into effect, the dockers were paid a minimum weekly wage of £20 whether or not there was work. The Aberdeen Stevedoring Company was formed in 1966 from an amalgamation of nine employers. Only one remains – John Cook and Sons Limited. Aberdeen Stevedoring Company and Cooks are now virtually synonymous.

From its inception to the present day, Aberdeen dock work has changed from being related to cargoes indigenous to the area such as grain, paper pulp, esparto-grass timber, cement, through the frenetic activity of the 1970s when everything revolved around North Sea oil and meeting its demands on a 24-hour service call, to the recession of recent years when dockers have been severely under-utilized.

The structure of the company in Autumn 1986 was 119 dockers and eight management staff, two wage clerks and a part-time invoice clerk, a mechanic, and two storemen. Retired dockers looked after the 'bothies', which are one permanent and one temporary hut provided for 'free time'.

An average of 100 men are available after deducting those who are on holiday, or sick, etc. The hours of work for everyone are 8 a.m. to 5 p.m. Monday to Thursday, and 8 a.m. to 4 p.m. Friday, with a 12 to 1 midday break, and 15 minutes break mid morning and afternoon. Each stevedore has a number. They meet at the National Dock Labour Board Hall at 7.45 a.m. and 12.00 noon and are allocated to work in a rota system to either the North Boat – 20 men – or to oil supply work which is supervised by foremen from oil companies, or to general cargo. Overtime is voluntary depending on work but there is a standby system for nights and weekends – 79 men at any one time are on retainer, with the rota being changed fortnightly. Five management staff supervise this operation, and are on call one week in every five. Stevedores who are called out are off the following day from 1 p.m. to 5 p.m.

Relationships are fraught with difficulties. Recruitment and discipline are contributory factors and are handled by committees which are virtual anachronisms from the pre-Devlin era.

There is a Registration Committee of two employers and two dockers which is responsible for work recruitment. The actual number who are recruited is dependent on trade and natural wastage. Twelve dockers were recruited in 1982. Applications are made in writing and marked by committee members on a 0–10 scale. In practice, this means virtually a closed-shop policy. Most stevedores are related.

The National Dock Labour Board services a committee to deal with all issues of grievance, discipline, and safety. The committee is composed of two Aberdeen Stevedoring Company managers, one Aberdeen Fish Landing Company manager, two dockers, and one fish market porter. In effect, this means dockers virtually have a job for life since any discipline is negated by the structure of the committee. Suspensions are sometimes applied and can vary from one to five days, depending on misdemeanours, with appropriate loss of pay.

A recent severance scheme funded by the government has seen the number of dockers drop from 119 in September 1986 to 91 in March 1987. The average wage in 1986 was £21,000. Severance pay after 15 years' service is £25,000 plus appropriate superannuation and pension. The diminishing amount of work which is available is now contributing to a change in entrenched attitudes and dockers' representatives are taking into consideration dual responsibilities with management for health and safety and considering possible disciplinary measures.

Fact finding on the docks and the need for action

Over a period of two and a half months in 1986, and not always drinking alcohol, I visited most of the 37 pubs in the area, together with eight licensed restaurants, two hotels, and sixteen off-licences. There are also several private clubs with subsidized prices not subject to police surveillance. Several public houses have extended licensing hours. Some are open at 7 a.m., others at 9 a.m., and many after 11 p.m. The rationale for early opening is to allow workers coming off night shift to have a drink on their way home. Most customers at 7 a.m. said to the bar staff: 'just in for my morning', 'what a night! – need a pick up', 'bloomin' cauld this morning', or such chat. Lunchtime entertainment is varied – ranging from folk singing to gogo dancers. Bars serve a wide range of food and alcohol is consumed as though it might go out of fashion. The clientele comes from right across the social board and the premises themselves range from old 'spilt and sawdust', through 'old oak twee', to up-market plush, with client groups from gays to last-bastion male chauvinists, with definite rendezvous spots for picking up whatever is one's sexual preference. The fact that from 7 a.m. to 5.00 p.m. most people on the docks are drinking and working did not seem to cause concern.

On 10 July, in the middle of this fact finding, I met with the Dock Labour Board Safety Committee to discuss the 'writing' of a policy. From the knowledge I had already gleaned I was able to establish rapport and credibility with both management and men and so suggested as an alternative that we could hold alcohol awareness sessions with all the company.

The aims and objectives were to achieve a base level knowledge of alcohol, afford an opportunity to discuss attitudes to alcohol use and misuse, to identify specific problems in the dock work situation, and then, if possible, to draft a policy with input from all. The rationale for this approach was that I had seen many policies written with the best of intentions but which had never been used, since no overall philosophy had even been discussed, and no alcohol awareness sessions or practical training done with the staff who had particular roles to play.

Management and men discussed my suggestions with their colleagues. Whilst it was not received with wild enthusiasm, there was no howl of dissent. It was agreed that sessions would be held in the Medical Centre from 9 to 11 a.m., and attendance would be voluntary. Tuesdays and Thursdays were targeted as days when work schedules were low, and more people would be able to attend.

The nursing sister went into the NDLB Hall at rota time in the first week of September 1986 and told the dockers, already briefed by their representatives, that the sessions would be starting the following week. She clarified the aims of the exercise and asked for everyone's co-operation. She suggested they might all benefit from checking their own knowledge of alcohol and since any future policy would be for the benefit of all they should be involved in the planning.

The first session took place on Tuesday, 16 September 1986. Fourteen out of a possible fifteen dockers came. Such is the grapevine on the docks, that I was well aware that I had to grab their interest and involve them.

Complete with overhead acetates and handouts and my 'professional suit', I started. I explained the work and basic philosophy of AACS: that anyone who chooses to drink may be at risk. I went on to explain that studies had shown that problems come from intoxication and heavy, regular use and that only a very small percentage of drinkers are dependent. I stressed that in AACS, we rarely used the term 'alcoholic' and did not believe that there was a disease called 'alcoholism'. I was then challenged by one old docker who thought that the whole thing was a waste of time. He said that I had 'only been on the docks five minutes' and 'what the f****** hell' did I know about drinking? With cool restraint I pointed out that when I drove along the quay he had been loading pipes – I had not challenged his ability to perform his task since I knew he was a stevedore and afforded him the respect of knowing his job. I hoped he would afford me the same respect as an alcohol practitioner knowing my job – the reply was 'a'right, fair dos'.

A lively discussion then ensued on 'what are alcohol problems?' and a statistics handout was studied and discussed. To find out their knowledge, for fun, we tried a quiz and discussed a variety of issues arising from each question. These included:

Alcohol as a psycho-active depressant drug
Units of alcohol
Effects of alcohol
Absorption rates in/out
Hangover – myths
Next-day driving
Attitudes – family, friends, society
Attitudes – alcohol use
Problems – liver, lover, livelihood, legal
Types of drunk – amorous, aggressive, maudlin, morose, sick
Scottish culture/dockers' views/specific problems in their work situation
Work situation – manual dexterity
– reasoning/memory
– accidents
– absence/time lost on job
How a company policy might work
'Covering up'

Workplace sanctions
Their views

The two hours passed quickly and feedback at the end was good.

Participants all admitted to having views that were expressed, but went away 'thinking'. Subsequent impressions gained by the nursing sister and management were – 'it's worth going'.

The eight further sessions covered much the same ground but with variations relating to the particular interests of group members in specific sections of the presentation. Discussions were frank. Men admitted to drink problems. Management and men had real 'ding-dongs' regarding bothy conditions and lots of lively and forthright statements were expressed.

I learned that standards varied depending on the foremen. For example, it was reported that there was no drinking on the North Boat. Grain loading, by contrast, was seen as an excuse for a drink – it was hot/cold work, dangerous when trimming, and decidedly thirst-making. Salvage boat owners brought a case of beer as compensation. Dockers at oil bases were under the supervision of oil company foremen who sometimes would not even enforce the wearing of hard hats, and in order to get a squad would use anyone regardless of their condition. Some stevedoring company and oil company foremen might even call a docker out of a pub aware he was intoxicated, to make up numbers. Views as to problem drinking varied. Policies were useless if 'they' wouldn't help themselves. I was asking men to sack themselves. How could they not drink on standby? The bothies were not big enough – no facilities, cold – the pub was the only place to go. What if friends came in when you were at home on standby? – you couldn't give them 'two large' and not drink yourself. Anyway, how many of them had a problem? – shock-horror reaction to estimate of 25 per cent from the nurse.

Policy discussions focused on who were to be the designated officers. How could you tackle a mate/friend? – they would never speak to you again. The great stumbling block was discipline. We argued whether it was fair to have different standards. What did covering up do – help or hinder? Had they individual responsibility, e.g. on call-out having been paid a retainer? Did they like doing extra work when a squad depleted? What about danger to oneself and to others?

A total of 108 out of the 119 dockers and eight management staff chose to attend the sessions. Discussions were then held with the Safety Committee and with a representative of the managing director and the director of the Aberdeen Stevedoring Company. These resulted in management agreeing to have a policy and uniform standards and the men conforming to them. Plans for a new large bothy were drawn up and decisions were made about the further training needs of those chosen to be designated officers and enforcing standards at oil company bases.

After discussion with the Safety Committee, a draft policy was tabled. It has now been approved by the Transport and General Workers' Union and is being studied by the National Dock Labour Board locally and nationally.

Locally discussion now centres round who are to be designated officers and how best their further training can be delivered. In the interim period there have been several voluntary and disciplinary referrals from the workforce to AACS. The Aberdeen scheme is being observed with great interest by the National Dock Labour Board.

Confidentiality in this workforce is non-existent. Everyone knows most of everybody else's lifestyle and problems. Attitudes have altered somewhat and it will be interesting to chart developments in the future. One interesting feature is that the Aberdeen Stevedoring Company is totally male orientated, no equal opportunities would ever be contemplated. Yet quite significant input has been achieved by the influence of two women – the Nursing Sister and me.

A 'soft' approach to industry

Ken Painter

In 1984, an 'Understanding Alcohol' programme of education was launched in the South West. The then Health Education Council (HEC) provided 'pump priming' funding and the local Councils on Alcoholism, and all the health districts in the South-West Region, plus Bath and West Dorset (which were also covered by the two independent TV stations in the South West) were invited to participate. It quickly became clear that additional staff were needed to make the programme a success. The HEC offered to fund half the salary costs of an alcohol co-ordinator for three years in each of the participating health districts. Because of the level of expertise in the alcohol field already possessed by existing staff, Southmead Health Authority did not take up this offer but, after discussions with John Teller, the Director of the Avon Council on Alcoholism, the two organizations decided to make a joint bid for an equivalent sum of money to be used to fund work with industry and with teenage motorcyclists. This article describes the work we have undertaken so far with four local industries.

Background to the approach

John Teller and I share the same philosophy regarding approaches to industry and commerce. Both of us have found that a 'high profile' approach, which starts from the premise that a company should prepare a policy on alcohol and work, has failed more often than it has succeeded. We agree that such an approach fails for one or more of the following reasons:

the company is not convinced that alcohol is a problem, or even a potential problem, among the workforce;

alcohol workers try to impose their own timetable for progress and ignore the process and structures within the company which influence the rate of progress which can be achieved. Cases are known where attempts to promote the concept of an alcohol policy were made during internal managerial reorganizations, boardroom changes, or industrial action;

policy statements are brief and often vague, with no clear guidelines for implementation;
policies are preparèd without any real commitment at the highest management level;
the policy document is drafted without consultation or discussion with union or shopfloor representatives;
there is no programme of training for managers or supervisors to equip them with the knowledge and skills needed to administer the policy;
there is no workforce education or publicity, so staff are unaware of the need for the alcohol policy, or of the way it should operate;
managers assume that alcohol problems are obvious, simply because they are a 'medical' matter;
managers are frequently reluctant to challenge the drinking behaviour of subordinates because they fear that their own drinking may be challenged;
alcohol policies frequently conflict with other existing company policies, such as those dealing with discipline.

We had both worked with industry before and had both used an approach which was geared more to the individual company's own perception of its needs. Pooling our experiences of successful approaches, we agreed on the following 'menu' of alcohol-related material and activities from which companies can pick whatever they feel is most appropriate to their situation:

posters, leaflets, and other materials designed to meet the company's individual needs;
articles for the 'in-house' magazine or newspaper;
advice to managers, supervisors, or occupational health staff;
input on induction courses;
special training for managers, supervisors, union and staff representatives, and occupational health staff;
advice and assistance on preparing and implementing an 'alcohol and work' policy, including any training required.

All these services were to be free to the company with the costs being met from the HEC grant.

John Teller had already established a close working relationship with the regional offices of the CBI and the TUC. Both were contacted to see if an introduction could be arranged with local industries. We wanted to reach as varied a range of companies as possible and our ideal mix would have included a large company, a medium-sized company, a small company, and a public body. The response from both the CBI and the TUC was extremely positive and helpful; indeed, it seemed to us at times that each was striving to better the attempts of the other. Eventually, through the good offices of the CBI, we were given the names of four companies who had agreed to see us. They included a large company of some 5,500 staff, involved in the aerospace industry, a chemicals company with some 750 staff on two adjacent sites, an engineering company with 150 staff, and a warehousing company with 50 staff.

Working with the four companies

Our approach was the same for all four companies. We wrote to arrange to visit each location, stressing in our letter that, since they had agreed to see us, we were not, in any way, suggesting that there was an alcohol problem within their workforce. The companies had clearly been briefed by the CBI representative before our visit and our host each time was a senior member of the company. One was the managing director, two were personnel directors, each of whom was accompanied by a personnel officer, and the fourth was the personnel manager, one of the senior executives based at that particular site.

The initial visit followed a common pattern. We introduced ourselves and described briefly the organizations we represented. We then explained in more detail the reason for our interest in them within the context of the South-West Regional Alcohol Programme. The response in every case was the same: 'we do not have a problem with alcohol at work.' Our reply was simply to state that we hoped to help them maintain this admirable record. As the conversation progressed, it often became clear that the company either did have a problem with staff who drank to excess, or had experienced such problems in the past. It also became clear that, in most cases, there were no company guidelines to help managers to deal with alcohol problems when they arose.

The first company we visited told us that management were concerned about the fact that shopfloor staff often elected to take their lunch break in local pubs, rather than use the company canteen. Further questioning revealed that they operated a series of canteens and staff restaurants for differing levels of staff and, as the seniority level increased, the availability of alcohol also increased, and the price decreased. The discussion that followed helped the company managers to recognize that they were applying different standards to differing levels of staff and helped to emphasize the point that alcohol was an issue which could affect staff at all levels within the company.

In our discussions we also stressed to the company that alcohol was often not even considered as a possible contributory cause of the problems. For example, they had been investigating possible reasons for an above-average accident rate when using hire cars for long journeys and had taken into account such varied factors as the effect of the sun as drivers drove east in the early morning, or west in the evening, or the fact that drivers would be less familiar with the controls of a hired car. But they had not considered whether the driver may have been drinking in the hours before the accident.

Our offer of the 'menu' of services was gratefully accepted and supplies of leaflets and posters were provided. They also suggested that we should prepare some articles for their company magazine. It transpired that the company was expecting a new managing director in the very near future, so we suggested that we wait until he was in post before we attempted any further work together. Shortly after this, our 'contact' with the company was taken ill and this slowed down our progress still further as it was felt that we should wait until he returned to work. However, contact has been maintained, and we have recently been asked to talk to new trainees about the costs and benefits of alcohol.

The second company we visited had already identified from their own staff records that a number of staff had been referred to the Avon Council on Alcoholism for counselling. We assured them that we were not there to talk about these people, but wished to discuss the wider issue of alcohol and the workplace. The company operated a shift working system and ran an on-site staff club, which served alcoholic drinks. They were aware of the potential dangers of staff drinking unwisely before the start of their shift, but emphasized that, to their knowledge, no such problems had occurred in the past.

As before, they were offered the 'menu' of services and they asked for information on the costs to industry due to alcohol abuse to be given to their health and safety committee. If the committee accepted that alcohol was a health and safety issue, we were to be asked to assist in the production of a small exhibition to be displayed for up to two months within the company. It is company practice to provide a new exhibition every other month, either on health and safety issues, or to publicize changes within the company. We provided the information and were to have produced a display for the spring, but a major reorganization of the company delayed this. At the time of writing no new date has been set for it, although the company keeps in regular contact with us to advise us of the progress of the reorganization.

The third company was a small warehousing organization, employing fifty staff. We were seen by the managing director, who was about to retire, but he assured us of the company's commitment to good staff relations. We were invited back to meet the new managing director shortly after he took up his post. He expressed keen interest in preparing a policy on alcohol and work because of his previous unhappy experiences in working with staff with serious alcohol problems. He felt that it would be appropriate to introduce such a policy after his own 'settling in' period. This would allow staff to get to know him and would allow for an atmosphere of trust to be built up. He was given some copies of alcohol policies prepared by other organizations and has now asked for a further meeting to discuss the preparation of an alcohol policy.

The fourth company visited employs about 150 staff on site. It is part of a larger, American-owned conglomerate and manufactures car and lorry steering assemblies. A few weeks before our visit, the American parent company had instructed all the companies within the group to prepare a policy on alcohol in the workplace and had provided a model policy for this purpose. As an American-owned company, there is a heavy emphasis on the employee assistance programme. A draft policy had been prepared, but the personnel manager expressed some reservations about it as he felt that it did little to meet the needs of the workforce. We offered assistance with the preparation and presentation of training programmes for staff and managers. So far, this offer has not been taken up.

What we have learned

On the face of it, very little progress has been made with any of the companies in this programme. But previous experience has shown that any attempt to involve industry in a dialogue about alcohol is a long-drawn-out affair. Alcohol is not perceived to be a major issue by the majority of companies and internal matters, such as staff changes, reorganizations, the winning or losing of contracts, industrial action by unions, and the like are issues that have to take priority.

It is our experience that visitors such as ourselves are subjected to a period of 'testing', when our professional competence and our ability to provide the benefits we offer are assessed. In the case of our four companies, this process is now over and we are able to demonstrate that we mean what we say. We have always stressed that we are prepared to work at the pace that suits the companies' particular circumstances, but show our commitment by regular informal contact to keep our channels of communication open. The companies have made good use of the materials and information we have provided. In two cases the numbers of clients referred to the Avon Council on Alcoholism have increased and this is acknowledged to be as a result of our contacts. Our goal is not simply a greater use of the treatment services, but a commitment to the positive benefits of an education and prevention programme within the workplace. For the four companies within our pilot programme this goal is now within reach.

Alcohol and professionals

Introduction

Not all alcohol problems require a professional response and the misplaced belief that they do has inhibited many non-professional groups from developing a helpful role. However, this is not to say that the contributions that professionals can make are unimportant. Far from it. Medical practitioners, nurses, social workers, probation officers, and other helping professionals clearly have central roles to play in the early identification of, and the provision of treatment for, individuals in difficulties. This was made very clear in the 1978 DHSS advisory committee report on *The Pattern and Range of Services for Problem Drinkers*. That report is still essential reading for participants in a local prevention strategy who wish to discuss the overall contribution which professionals can make, their relationship with non-specialist groups and agencies, and the development of the complex services in which they work.

The five contributions in this section testify to the scope that exists for professionals of all kinds to develop small-scale but significant and valuable local initiatives, thus creating a propitious climate for the further development of professional services in their area. The first chapter by Dr Tomson focuses on the vitally important issue of organizational records. Dr Tomson's chapter outlines the steps he took to create alcohol record cards in his practice. The existence of these cards has increased the 'visibility' of alcohol issues throughout the practice and reinforced and consolidated a 'risk factor' approach to alcohol, i.e. the routine asking of routine questions about alcohol consumption.

This chapter is particularly significant because, too often, discussions about how to put alcohol 'on the agenda' concentrate on awareness building and raising the level of individuals' knowledge and confidence. However, such strategies often fail to significantly alter organizational habits because the framework of everyday activity is not changed in tandem. If opportunities for 'thinking alcohol' are not a routine part of procedure and practice, there is little chance that the subject will become an organizational issue. It sometimes makes more sense to build up an organization's concern for the topic through small-scale changes to record cards, interview forms, schedules, check lists, and other documentation of all kinds, than to impose a concern from the top. What simple changes to which of your organization's records are feasible as the first step towards altering its priorities and concerns?

An example of how effective comparatively minor procedural changes can be is also provided by Dr Brooks' chapter. He outlines how one accident and emergency department has developed a system for providing patients with advice cards when it appears that alcohol is a factor in their presenting problem. Unlike Dr Tomson's initiative, the development of this advice card system required considerable preliminary negotiation and the allaying of fears among accident and emergency staff. This is not surprising. Even the smallest and simplest local prevention initiative will require considerable groundwork if its implementation requires the participation of a number of professional groups. However, like Dr Tomson's initiative, it too has led to changes in routines and the institutionalization of a concern for alcohol-related issues. This can only be beneficial not just for the patients who have, by virtue of the system, been prompted to seek advice but because such changes can provide a base for future policy developments.

Most helping professionals have to deal with alcohol-related problems every day, since alcohol consumption above a moderate level is a significant contributory factor in almost every situation in which harm is done by people to themselves or to each other, whether this is in relation to physical and mental health, family and social relationships, work, or the law. That this is not always fully recognized is due, in part, to a belief common to many occupational groups that they can do little to help people in difficulties with alcohol. Social workers are perhaps a specially disadvantaged group in that often their records, which can be used to unlock the door of organizational commitment, are deliberately rudimentary.

Peter Abel, a social worker and the author of the third chapter in this section, which describes the setting up of an alcohol advice centre, had no professional inhibitions when it came to devising a response to alcohol problems in his locality. His own research had given him an insight into the ubiquitous nature of alcohol problems among social service clients. Indeed, one of the most important points he makes in his chapter concerns the need for local projects and initiatives to be buttressed by some simple but telling research. Perhaps the most important aspect of the advice centre is that it was, and remains, a collaborative enterprise between a social services department and a local alcohol agency. Inter-agency collaboration has had important results. Social work clients and others have been helped. A better understanding of the 'alcohol dimension' of clients' problems has been fostered within the local social services department. Finally, the centre has stimulated other agencies to come and learn.

Doctors and social workers are not the only professionals who have an important role to play in responding to alcohol problems. This is clear from Rhona Panton's chapter which describes a pharmacy-based initiative designed to disseminate simple, practical alcohol education to customers. Nearly 10,000 leaflets were taken by customers, mostly women, over a three-week period. Pharmacies are clearly potentially very valuable outlets for information and advice of this sort since, as the project revealed, over 60 per cent of women and 35 per cent of men visit a pharmacy once a week or more. Addresses from where copies of the leaflet used and the final project report can be obtained are given in Panton's chapter. Hopefully, other localities will want to emulate this successful effort at public education.

The co-operation and the benefits that can flow from joint learning is the theme of the fifth and final chapter in this section by Dr John Bligh, who describes the formation and preliminary work of the Chester and Ellesmere Port Alcohol Forum. It aims to raise alcohol awareness among key professional groups and organizations within the locality, thereby encouraging the development of initiatives, fostering inter-agency collaboration, and preventing duplication of effort: in short, pressing for prevention.

This task is vitally important and every locality should have a local prevention group which can act as a focus for prevention concerns. As the chapters in this volume make clear, individuals and organizations can generate their own initiatives and self-sustaining commitment. However, these are exceptional. Were it otherwise, there would be no need to describe their work and encourage others to emulate the activities described. Given that many groups and organizations (i) believe they have little to contribute to a community prevention effort or (ii) that alcohol problems are no concern of theirs or (iii) that there is little they can do to help or (iv) that they are simply too busy to think constructively about the issue, it is clearly important that there should be a well-respected group encouraging them to learn about the problem and to do something constructive about it. The great danger, of course, is that such groups, whether based on existing bodies or constructed 'from scratch' like the Chester and Ellesmere Port Alcohol Forum, become simply 'talking shops' and platforms from which good intentions can be proclaimed but from which little else flows. This is clearly not the case with the group described in Dr Bligh's chapter which already has some substantial educational achievements to its credit. It is hoped that the initiatives outlined in this volume will both stimulate the development of other local groups prepared to press for prevention and provide them with models to promote either among their member organizations or, perhaps, on their own account. It is particularly important that professionals of every kind are represented on such groups and are willing to take the lead in pressing for prevention activities in their own and other organizations. They have the legitimacy, authority, and prestige needed to make things happen.

Reference

Report by the Advisory Committee on Alcoholism (1978) *The Pattern and Range of Services for Problem Drinkers*, London: DHSS.

General practitioner records and patients' alcohol use

Dr Peter Tomson

All general practitioners occasionally encounter patients with severe alcohol problems. I think my colleagues would agree that such people are difficult to help and treat and that most practitioners would seek to refer them on to more specialized sources of help. However, such cases are only the tip of the iceberg. I have been in practice for 33 years and it has become steadily more apparent that less acute, but still serious alcohol problems are relatively frequent among my patients if I look for them. This perception does not come easily to me since alcohol problems were not part of my medical education. However, two events served to bring home to me the extent of unhealthy and sometimes dangerous drinking among my patients. Quite by chance, in 1983, I became involved in a minor piece of research which used an alcoholmeter to screen patients for alcohol problems (Wiseman *et al.*, 1982: 1089–90).

The alcoholmeter was offered to every third patient at both morning and evening surgeries in four practices. One thousand patients were recruited and one in thirty had a positive test; many of these were overconsuming alcohol. Surprisingly only one patient refused to be tested and most were pleased that their doctor was interested in this aspect of their health.

After this was published, someone thought I must be an expert on alcohol problems in general practice and I was asked to join a Royal College of General Practitioners (RCGP) Working Party to produce a report on the subject (RCGP, 1986). As a result of these experiences I realized four things:

- I was unaware of the large number of patients who were drinking heavily and riskily, though I probably knew a fair proportion of those who were severely damaged and were damaging others;
- contrary to my belief, it is not too difficult to help people who are drinking heavily and riskily but who are not severely damaged;
- I needed more than good intentions if I was to help many people;
- helping many people with problems might be more effective than attempting (often unsuccessfully) to help a few with very severe problems.

I was determined to do something and to put into practice the interventions and techniques we had discussed on the Working Group and afterwards incorporated in its Report. However, it seemed to me that, in order to use these to the best effect, I had to have a record-system which matched my aspirations. The shape in which records are kept help us to define a problem, keep it in view, and monitor its progress. The importance of good record keeping is, of course, recognized by practitioners and if cards, such as antenatal cards, are used most doctors will complete them, perhaps because inside most of us there is a mildly obsessional person (could we pass finals if this were not true?).

In the 1970s, the nature of general practice changed from being an on-demand acute service, to one in which more emphasis needed to be given to the care of patients with chronic major illnesses such as hypertension, diabetes mellitus, and epilepsy. During this time, I designed and used special cards to help manage these diseases and to enable me to keep a constant check on such things as blood pressure levels. The experiment was very successful. For example, in the case of hypertension, the blood pressure of patients for whom special record cards were employed was maintained at a consistently lower level than in those who did not have such a record. This seems to have been both because the visual display made it easier to titrate the blood pressure against the medication and because sharing the card with the patient motivated them to comply with preventive advice. Sharing problems with patients encourages co-operation (Tomson, 1985: 534-5).

It seemed to me that since alcohol was associated with as much distress as the above diseases that we should put a similar amount of effort into introducing similar record cards for alcohol use. These would remind us to regularly ask questions about drinking behaviour and record both that behaviour and any advice or intervention we might think necessary.

The alcohol record card

The alcohol record card is part of a series of record cards used in our practice. When patients register they fill in a data-base card which records details of family history, past illnesses, and current alcohol intake. The top sheet of the notes is always a problem card which lists in a clear way current physical, psychological, and social problems and important past history. It is created by the doctor, when he first sees a patient, using some of the data from the data-base card but also information from the rest of the notes and from the patient. The reverse of the problem card provides structured space for serial information about preventive health issues which now also includes alcohol, and the information acts as a reminder to regularly ask about this issue. The alcohol record card is part of this comprehensive effort to identify and record patients' drinking behaviour and is created when it appears that a patient has a problem or runs a real risk of developing one.

FRONT

Alcohol Card

SURNAME	FORENAMES	D of B	SEX

DATE	ETHNIC ORIGIN

PRESENTING PROBLEMS

AMOUNT DRUNK/WEEK UNITS

PATTERN OF DRINKING

WHY MISUSING

HARMS

PHYSICAL
PSYCHOLOGICAL
BEHAVIOUR
FAMILY
SOCIAL

RISK FACTORS

OCCUPATION	PERSONALITY
FAMILY	TOBACCO
CULTURE	OTHER

FAMILY	FAMILY OF ORIGIN
MARITAL	
CHILDREN	CHILDHOOD

REVERSE

ATTEMPTS AT CONTROL	MAJOR ILLNESSES OTHER DRUGS
EXAMINATION WT. B.P.	INVESTIGATIONS GGT CHOL MCV OTHER BAL CREAT URATE

	DATE	DATE	DATE	DATE	DATE
PROBLEM NOT AGREED					
PROBLEM AGREED					
DECIDED ON ACTION					
ACTION IMPLEMENTED					

CONTRACT AND PLAN

ALCOHOL

HARM

FAMILY SEEN

DATE

CONTRACT

INVOLVED

HV	MGC
SW	AA
CAT	OTHER
ACS	
PSYCHOLOGIST	

 GPS 12

ALCOHOL CARD

The alcohol cards used in my practice are intended to be both a record of a patient's alcohol use and a reminder of the way in which the doctor may be able to help patients to understand not only that they have a problem but why and how it is maintained. There are two cards, the first, the Alcohol Card, records the initial assessment and the overall strategy. It seeks to collect basic information on alcohol use and it focuses on the disadvantages of misusing alcohol and its deleterious effects on the patient's body, mind, and social life. Merely collecting this kind of information can have a markedly beneficial impact. It also provides space for possible plans of management which might be agreed by the patient and doctor. The second card, the Alcohol Continuation Card, provides a record of the amount drunk per week and information about the current problems and management plan.

Part of my routine in every consultation involves opportunistic screening for alcohol problems if it has not been done recently. Whatever the reason for the consultation I ask patients how much they are drinking and initiate the alcohol card only if it is apparent that alcohol is being consumed riskily. However, I may not attempt to ask all the questions or to fully complete the

FRONT

ALCOHOL CONTINUATION CARD

SURNAME	FORENAMES	D of B	SEX

DATE	UNIT WEEK	GGT	MCV	BAL	PROBLEMS AND MANAGEMENT

REVERSE

DATE	UNIT WEEK	GGT	MCV	BAL	PROBLEMS AND MANAGEMENT

ALCOHOL CONTINUATION CARD

particular interview. Sometimes I delay the initiation until I can see the patient for a longer period. Any gaps that I may leave on the card act as a reminder for the next consultation. I am slowly introducing alcohol record cards in the following circumstances:

for all men who probably consume more than 50 units of alcohol per week;
for all women who probably consume more than 35 units of alcohol per week;
for all patients who have suffered significant harm due to the use of alcohol (more than the occasional harm than most of us have brought on ourselves by way of hangovers, broken glasses, and rows!);
for patients drinking 21–50 units of alcohol per week (men) and 16–35 units of alcohol per week (women) if (i) they have conditions such as diabetes, hypertension, or epilepsy, (ii) they are members of an 'at risk' group where alcohol consumption is concerned (barmen, salesmen, and doctors), and (iii) if they are in occupations where their drinking might put other people at risk (pilots, train drivers, and doctors).

Patients drinking in the 21–50 unit and 16–35 unit range without any apparent risk do not get alcohol cards but are offered blood tests for GTT and MCV, routine advice on drinking sensibly, and a copy of the Health Education Authority's *That's the Limit*. Their weekly alcohol consumption is recorded in their notes with a reminder to review the information in 12 months' time.

The approach can provide a springboard for other initiatives. Opportunistic screening is the basis of sound preventive health practice. We own a computer and in 1986 an opportunistic screening package was created. At most surgeries a list of patients attending is created together with details of preventive health measures outstanding. The doctor is thus reminded what to do and can enter action taken on the form which is then fed back to update the computer. It was easy to arrange for alcohol to be included in the package which provides yet another way of making questions about alcohol use routine and recording patients' drinking habits.

Advantages of the cards

They help to remind me that alcohol is a constant problem and to ask questions regularly that may help both the patient and myself to understand that problem. I often encourage patients to read parts of their notes including the alcohol record card. Sharing information in this way improves the doctor/patient relationship and encourages patient autonomy. The card allows us to formulate a joint plan for the patient's recovery and to monitor his or her progress. Should the doctor be sufficiently enthusiastic, the cards make the task of reviewing the care of patients with alcohol problems comparatively easy, thus acting as an encouragement to research. Finally, working with people with alcohol problems is not a solo effort; it usually involves the whole practice. Adequate notes and information for the rest of the primary care team is essential so that everyone knows who is involved, what we are doing, and why.

Disadvantages of the cards

Filling in the alcohol card takes time but I firmly believe that this is more than out-weighed by the time saved by identifying the problems at an early stage. Another more cogent objection is that general practice is (or should be) about whole person medicine. Dividing people's notes up by problem area may be unhelpful and prevent us from identifying other issues that the patient brings to the consultation. I suspect that practitioners with a very strong commitment to the holistic approach may well find the idea of separate record cards for separate problem areas unattractive. Nevertheless, I believe the advantages outweigh the disadvantages and have found them invaluable in educating my patients about alcohol and helping those who are at risk to drink sensibly. Finally, although the card puts alcohol routinely on the consultation agenda, the checklist of questions may cramp one's thinking and limit decision-making. This is a risk with any procedure or record system. However, the answer is surely not to abandon the system but to improve it in ways that one feels appropriate. I am sure other practitioners could improve on my design.

Conclusion

I have been using alcohol record cards for over a year, but sadly, I have not kept a list of those patients for whom an alcohol card has been issued. I would recommend any practitioners adopting my approach to keep a separate list for their own record and research purposes.

The computer has only just begun to record morbidity and I am not in a position at the moment to discover how many patients we have identified drinking riskily. A recent manual search of a sample of the records has shown that in 59 per cent of the notes of adults over 16 years of age, the intake has been recorded on the preventive health section of the card. All the partners and nurses have accepted the importance of alcohol information on the data-base and problem cards and of opportunistic screening for health prevention generally but, as yet, I am the only one using the alcohol record cards. Change takes time. The alcohol cards and problem cards (and diabetic, hypertension, and epilepsy cards) may be obtained from G.P.S Supplies, 314 St Albans Rd., Watford, Herts. (Watford (0923) 42128).

References

RCGP (1986) *Alcohol – A Balanced View*, Report from General Practice No. 24, London: Royal College of General Practitioners.

Tomson, P. (1985) *Sharing Problem Cards With Patients*, No. 35, London: RCGP.

Wiseman, S.D., Tomson, P.R.V., Barrett, J.M., Jenns, M., and Wilton, J. (1982) 'The Use of an Alcoholmeter to Detect Problem Drinkers', *British Medical Journal* 285: 1089–90.

A & E advice cards for problem drinkers

Dr S.C. Brooks

Patients with alcohol-related conditions present frequently in accident and emergency (A and E) departments. The presentation may be due to injury sustained while under the influence of alcohol, the result of altercations when the participants were drunk, or the result of assault to which those who have drunk to excess seem more vulnerable. There are also, of course, road accidents caused by drunk driving and drunk pedestrians who stagger into the road. It is important to treat not only the presenting problem but also the underlying cause. Failure to recognize and respond to the 'alcohol dimension' is as regrettable as treating the infected foot of a diabetic without picking up the diabetes! In our accident unit attempts are made to counsel and refer for help anyone with a drink problem who is willing to accept the offer. However, it is not always possible to raise and discuss the issue in a sensible way. Some patients will maintain their defences and deny they have a problem. Others may be suffering from the after-effects of drink or agree with everything that is said if they are shocked and upset by their injuries or, in some cases, need a bed for the night. Consequently, a card system was designed by a group including alcohol unit staff, social workers, and a physician with an interest in alcohol-related pathology, to reach those not prepared at the time of presentation to accept referral or discussion.

The 'green card'

Accident units traditionally hand out information relating to injuries and/or treatment given. Thus, patients with head injuries are given a 'head injury advice card' when discharged, advising them of symptoms to watch out for which indicate a need to return. We designed a simple card to be given to patients when we felt alcohol was a significant factor in their presentation. The aim was to alert them to this fact and offer details of local help available. We took great care over the wording on the card to avoid offending or alienating those who have drunk to excess on a single occasion such as a stag night or 21st birthday party. We did not want to devalue the exercise by having people frame the card as a memento of the occasion! The card, which measures

4.5" × 4", is given to patients when they leave the department and advises them that 'We are concerned that your attendance at Casualty on ...... involved excessive alcohol consumption on that occasion. You may wish to discuss this with someone in confidence – your G.P. or any of the following:'

It is printed on one side only in black and is known colloquially as the 'green card' because of its colour. The card is given to certain categories of patient when they leave the department. We decided the cards were to be given to the following groups:

- all patients requiring admission primarily because of alcohol intake;
- all patients with a breath alcohol greater than 200 mg per cent;
- patients presenting after drinking at an inappropriate time of day, i.e. morning or while at work;
- patients whom the attending staff felt, for any reason, had an alcohol problem.

When a card is issued a letter is sent to the patient's G.P. drawing their attention to their patient's alcohol use. The letter has a space for the patient's name and then simply goes on to state that 'Your patient's attendance at Casualty on ..... appears to have involved excessive alcohol consumption. Breathalyser at .... was...... It is possible that there is a problem which may require help. If you feel that help is required the following agencies are available.....'

The level of 200 mg per cent was set after much discussion. Some members of the planning group were surprised to hear from A and E staff that a level set at 150 mg per cent would include a large proportion of the patients attending on a Saturday night – no doubt including at times many of the planners or their colleagues! The inclusion of a breath alcohol criteria involved extending the use of a breathalyser already employed in the department. This device had caused considerable anxiety among hospital staff when first introduced, perhaps because they sometimes identified with the casualties knowing they also drank possibly to excess at times; and also because of the medico-legal concerns. After discussion with the Medical Defence Union (MDU) and the police it was made clear that levels taken by medical staff for use as part of the medical assessment of a patient cannot be used against them in court – even if the notes are subpoenaed at a later date. This is because breath tests taken for police use in court must be taken under strict conditions of signed consent. If the forms are not signed the results cannot be used in court. Other than this contact, the police were not involved in the project in any way which was seen purely as a medical treatment initiative. With these reassurances, junior staff are encouraged to breathalyse any patient they think may have been drinking as part of their assessment – particularly in the case with head injuries.

Patients very rarely show resentment either to the breath test or the cards. If there is any problem then we do not insist on either. The first batch of cards were financed by research funds from the alcohol unit at the local psychiatric hospital. We now have them printed as a standard hospital stationery issue.

After extending the use of the breathalyser as part of the green card scheme we became aware that several young male attenders, who had been involved in road traffic accidents, were delaying attendance in A and E until the following day if they had been drinking. This delay in receiving treatment was a serious cause for concern and, if it had continued, would have altered our management. However, we lost no opportunity to get patients to understand that the results were for medical and not legal use and fortunately this delay in attendance has now stopped. We now see patients as close to the time of accidents as before.

Another early and interesting proof that the cards were being noted was an approach from Alcoholics Anonymous (AA) asking why their name and phone number were not on the card. This was because of our desire to assess the usefulness of the card by monitoring numbers presenting to the help agency listed. We knew that because of their total confidentiality rules, AA would not supply us with names of clients and we would not therefore know if patients were presenting to two agencies at once. However, we have now added AA to the card.

Impact

We experienced the usual problems in persuading junior staff to record details of cards given out. In the first six months some 250 cards were given but details of only fifty were recorded although this situation has steadily improved with encouragement. However, of those cards we did record, we were surprised and very pleased to find a 30 per cent presentation rate at one or another agency – some after a delay of many months. Agencies notify us of presentations by quoting the green card number. Most were new self-referrals to the agencies but some were previous attenders, prompted by the card to present again after a period of thought following the A and E attendance. In at least one case, the card was found by a relative in the patient's pocket and the resultant family discussion of a previously unrecognized problem persuaded him or her to attend.

We have been more than satisfied that the cards have a useful part to play in persuading those who do not drink sensibly to recognize they may have a problem and to seek help. We have continued their use and are currently issuing about 500 every six months. Interest has been shown by other areas and a locally relevant card can easily be designed and printed. It should be pocket sized and durable, as our experience has shown that it may be some time before a patient finally makes contact with a helping agency.

Establishing an advice centre

Peter M. Abel

As a social worker it had long been obvious to me that many of the problems with which I was required to deal involved alcohol misuse. Certain family problems which persisted over time could not be explained in any other way and, once appropriate and relevant questions were put to family members, alcohol often emerged as the important factor in their difficulties. This created difficulties for me, as it does for many social workers. I had received no training in this subject area on my professional qualifying course; there was no in-service training available, and my colleagues and managers lacked knowledge and experience of working in this area. Although there was 'sympathetic' interest concerning clients with alcohol problems, it was not viewed by my department as a 'priority' area, nor had any policy been formulated concerning any aspect of substance abuse generally, whether concerning clients or for staff.

Although the situation has improved considerably in recent years, social workers in many areas still suffer from a lack of training in this vital area and lack of organizational commitment. For instance, before an organization can help others with alcohol problems its members have to be prepared to sort out their own attitude towards alcohol and be prepared to help themselves. This can be done through the adoption of comprehensive workplace policies, but how many Social Services Departments (SSDs) have such a policy?

My involvement

My interest in this dimension of family case-work brought me into contact with my local Council on Alcoholism. Where they exist, these organizations are a vital resource for social workers not only for referrals but also as a source of advice and support which may be lacking in their own organizations. I was drawn into training activities which turned my interest from a purely personal one into a concern to develop practical initiatives, which would help social workers facing similar problems with their case-loads. Consequently, I took the decision to pursue a Personal Social Services Fellowship to research a problem area which was clearly both relevant to my department and to university. The latter proved no problem as a recommended tutor already displayed an active interest in alcohol abuse. However, the department proved more difficult to convince.

Problems of absence were relatively easily overcome as colleagues were supportive of my proposal and recognized the possible pay-offs for their own work. It also helped that I was a long-term serving member of the district. The real problem was convincing the training section at head office that the subject area was relevant and that the research would benefit the department in a practical manner. Luckily, similar research had been carried out in Lothian, Scotland (Leckie *et al.*, 1981) which showed that a high percentage of family cases researched were alcohol-related and that lack of departmental policy and training can lead to inadequate assessment and intervention by social workers, thus prolonging the 'vicious circle'. Armed with these results and various DHSS circulars and publications, I was able to argue the case. Anyone in a similar position must be similarly well prepared and able to argue a cogent case. It might also help to argue, as I did, that the research would only be worthwhile if it was followed by some form of practical initiative. I believe that this argument was an important factor in my department agreeing to the proposed research and led on to the establishment of the South Bristol Alcohol Advice Centre.

The results of my research (Abel, 1983; 1987: 12–13) confirm the Lothian studies and take the findings a step further. Concentrating on current family cases held by four teams of social workers in South Bristol the research confirmed that social workers attempt to deal with a whole range of problems which persist over time without seeing their relationship to alcohol abuse. The multiple problems experienced by families where alcohol abuse exists are of the same kind as social workers see in other families where alcohol is not a problem. I identified a number of 'key clues' to which social workers must be alert if they are to recognize the true nature of the presenting problems. Some of the key clues are intoxication, clients smelling of drink, and the observation of withdrawal symptoms, e.g. hand tremors. Others involving information on family drinking behaviour must be actively sought from family members themselves or other professionals and involved agencies. Without a proactive and inquiring stance social workers will remain in their own 'vicious circle' in which a lack of departmental policy and low or non-existent levels of training lead inexorably to low levels of recognition and, hence, the maintenance of clients' own 'vicious circle'.

Setting up the Advice Centre

The original agreement that the research project would be followed, if at all possible, by some form of practical initiative led to the proposal that the department become actively involved in providing a counselling service to encourage more referrals from social workers and thus indirectly increase their levels of awareness, interest, and commitment. This was done by means of a joint arrangement with the Avon Council on Alcoholism which resulted in the establishment of South Bristol Alcohol Advice Centre. Social Services (South Bristol) provide a shop-fronted local sub-office premises for half a day a week between 1 p.m. and 6 p.m. and I spent one-fifth of my time managing/counselling at the Centre. Another enthusiastic social worker was allowed one-tenth of her time. The Avon Council on Alcoholism manages the referral system. The Council also provides administrative support plus two trained volunteer counsellors. Negotiations to set up the Alcohol Advice Centre were not easy since social work time was involved. In particular, a redistribution of case-loads to compensate for work taken on at the Centre was discussed at length. The proposal was viewed sympathetically but in the end proved impossible to implement. The fact that there was no drain on area funds was a key factor in the department's agreement to the project. All resources that were used were either given, begged, or borrowed from Social Services and the Avon Council on Alcoholism. A contract was agreed by both services and this contained a built-in review system, but it did not allow for any expansion of social work input nor did it allow for replacement of any staff. The South Bristol Alcohol Advice Centre became operational in 1984.

The centre in action

Since the Advice Centre opened it has warranted the effort. The Advice Centre serves the function of a focal point for both social workers and clients. Social workers and students are able to visit the premises to gain advice and information with reference to clients' alcohol problems. Clients were able to visit the Centre with the knowledge that any information is confidential and will only be given to Social Services if agreed. In this way a joint but independent alcohol service is made available to both professionals and customers in the community. Before 1984 social services' referrals to the Council on Alcoholism fluctuated around 5 per cent of all referrals per year. In the first two years of operation, Social Service referrals to the South Bristol Centre averaged 40 per cent. This dropped by 5 per cent in following years after the initial flooding of 'sticky' long-term cases had filtered through the system. There have also been no shortage of referrals from clients directly as the Centre became better known. An alcohol input on the university social work course became an annual event. Professional visits to the Centre have been numerous, ranging from students on various courses to the local police, community and youth workers, and members of the health professions. Unfortunately, despite hard work, the Centre failed to attract referrals or visits by local G.P.s, with a couple of notable exceptions. However, strong referral links have been made with the local alcohol teaching centre and health visitors have proved to be most useful allies and the source of many referrals. Visitors have been given information on the work of the Centre, with counselling and assessment techniques and evaluation of the extent of the problem in the local community.

For the client the benefits have been considerable and alone justify the nature and work of the joint project. Confidentiality is set at a premium and, unlike attending an area office, identity does not have to be revealed. Case-notes are kept as brief and concise as possible, and the content relevant and open to the client. Joint working between the client, counsellor, and social worker is encouraged and the clients benefit from sessions with the counsellor at which alcohol problems can be discussed without being tied to statutory or departmental considerations. Social workers benefit as they concentrate on those related problems, such as financial mismanagement and child behaviour, which until then had persisted over time. Fast referral links to other specialist agencies have been forged while contacts with community groups such as Alcoholics Anonymous have been established. The basic philosophy underlying the project is pragmatic rather than philosophical – every effort is made to offer a wide choice of options to clients deciding how to tackle their problem.

Alongside these developments a South Bristol Addiction Support Group has been established for social work staff. Like all departmental support groups its future will depend on the time and energy hard-pressed social workers will be able to give to enable it to grow and influence department procedures and policy. On a wider community level the Advice Centre with the Avon Council on Alcoholism helped establish the South Bristol Forum on Alcohol Problems. The Forum is open to all interested members of the community, both lay and professional. Initially, and perhaps inevitably, the Forum has mainly attracted a small group of already committed professionals, but the Forum has scored enormously by annually organizing a Youth and Health Exhibition which attracts a significant number of the young from local schools and colleges. These three main areas of progress in South Bristol have gone a long way in keeping the problems of alcohol use and abuse in high profile to the local community. There is no doubt in my mind that the experience has been positive for all those involved, but there are still lessons to be learned.

Conclusions: the benefits of hindsight

Among the lessons learned from the experience were, first, that if social workers are to be seconded to such a project then guidelines on how their work time is to be split between project and departmental responsibility must be made clear. If this is not done a problem can develop for the social worker who on the one hand is drawn more and more to the specialist work but on the other is pulled back to statutory duties. The contract needs to be clear in the nature of the secondment.

Second, if the project is to grow from the experimental stage it requires an independent budget. Hence an evaluative system needs to be implemented from the outset which will supply the necessary data to support an application for future finances. Such a system requires extra staff time and effort and should be noted in seconded time.

Third, although the Centre received enthusiastic support from local social services management the response from higher up the structure was not always supportive. Avenues of communication need to be opened between the levels of management within the department to help secure future funding and policy formation.

All these points are obvious with hindsight. At the time, the reality of the situation was that we launched the project with all the available support and resources that we could muster and the gains outweighed the problems that emerged later. The experience revealed the usefulness of research in mobilizing resources to initiate a practical response. Research does not have to be complicated or time-consuming. Simple, local surveys linking alcohol problems with other problem areas, such as child abuse, can reveal useful motivating information. The project proved the usefulness of linking with the specialist voluntary sector, a source in this case of continued support and immense expertise. Most areas possess a local voluntary agency which deals with alcohol problems. These agencies are usually more than willing to supply support, advice, and training. Lastly, the idea of local forums of people who share a common concern about a community problem is gaining in popularity. Forum issues can be wide ranging from lack of local community care for a group of homeless drinkers to national issues concerning drinking and driving.

The South Bristol Alcohol Advice Centre has provided important lessons for social workers. Working with alcohol problems requires the same skills as working in other problem areas. Training designed to enhance confidence is important and must be developed as a preparation for, and as an adjunct to, an initiative of this kind. Alcohol problems affect all social work client groups including children, young people, families, the elderly, and the handicapped. You will find colleagues in all these areas of work who may wish to form an alcohol support group which can then be used to underpin specific initiatives.

The British Association of Social Work (BASW) Addictions Working Party has published guidelines for social service departments and this could serve as a focus for alcohol support group formation. Local research is important. This need not be complicated. Straightforward team or area surveys linking alcohol misuse to various client problem areas, such as the Child Abuse Register and the elderly, can help motivate staff and encourage local training and other alcohol initiatives. Links with your local alcohol agencies are vitally important. Most areas of the country possess some form of voluntary alcohol agency which will be eager to offer support, advice, and information. Get in touch with them and share your worries, experiences, and expertise.

References

Abel, P. (1983) *Alcohol Related Problems in Current Social Work Cases*, Personal Social Services/Bristol University Fellowship Research Project.

Abel, P. (1987) 'How social workers can help break the vicious circle', *Social Work Today* 18, 19: 12–13.

Leckie, T. *et al.* (1981) *Alcohol Problems in Current Cases*, Edinburgh: Lothian Region Social Work Department.

Pharmacy-based advice for drinkers

Rhona Panton

In 1986 the Alcohol and Pharmacy Action Groups of the West Midlands Regional Health Authority's (RHA) Advisory Group on Health Promotion joined forces to mount a moderate drinking programme in twenty-one pharmacies in Wolverhampton and Shropshire. The intention was to assess the best ways pharmacies could be used to give information on alcohol problems, and also to profile pharmacy customers. The pharmacists were not expected to counsel people on drinking problems but to answer questions of fact and offer the addresses of local agencies, such as Aquarius.

Pharmacies were chosen for the project for two reasons. First, because of the success of previous pharmacy-based projects on smoking and heart disease which had established that, by giving pharmacies a simple *aide-mémoire* to pin on the dispensary wall, we could change their advice-giving behaviour from a great range of possible statements to three specific pieces of advice. Second, people do not, of course, have to become patients to ask a pharmacist for advice. The pharmacies selected gave a good spread of urban and rural areas and both areas could offer support services such as Aquarius or Alcoholics Anonymous (AA) for people who might need help. The programme was monitored by a research worker who discussed progress with the pharmacists and interviewed them and their customers.

The pharmacy advice project

The project ran for eight weeks during which 286 customers were interviewed on their awareness of the alcohol material displayed, their drinking habits, and the kinds of health problems for which they would seek help and advice from a pharmacist. Four leaflets were used in the moderate drinking programme. Two of these were specially designed for the project.

The first of these specially designed leaflets was bottle shaped with a pull-out tab which revealed the legal and medical consequences of drinking different amounts. The second leaflet was devoted to medicines and alcohol and was designed to give specific information on this important topic. This leaflet emphasized that alcohol is a drug, made the point strongly that medicines and alcohol may be a dangerous mixture, and listed some of the conditions where the interaction of drugs and alcohol may be unwise and even dangerous. Copies of the latter leaflet can be obtained from Gill Synnott, West Midlands RHA, Newland House, 139 Hagley Road, Birmingham, B16 8UA. We also used the excellent Health Education Authority's (HEA) booklet *That's the Limit* and *Basic Facts*, designed and produced by the Teachers' Advisory Council on Alcohol and Drug Education (TACADE). (Both these booklets are available from the HEA at Hamilton House, Mabledon Place, London WC1H 9TX.) Pharmacists' awareness of alcohol problems and the legal and medical results of excessive drinking too much were pre-tested and they were found to be well informed.

Nearly 10,000 leaflets were taken by customers during the programme which lasted three weeks. This averaged about 500 from each pharmacy – although the average was higher in Wolverhampton, where many of the outlets were in deprived areas. The important point was that all of them were taken by people in the community who did not have to become patients to get the information. Pharmacists agreed that young-to-middle-aged women took most of the leaflets, often commenting that they were for someone else. Women customers, who do most of the shopping, are clearly a means of communicating with families and of influencing behaviour since, as market research emphasizes, they are important as domestic opinion leaders.

Some pharmacists thought it was better to offer leaflets, on what could be an embarrassing subject, in a rack with others on different subjects, from where they could be taken more discreetly. Several pharmacies in Wolverhampton asked for leaflets in Asian languages but a nationwide search found none – nor any counsellors on alcohol problems who speak any Indian language. A separate survey conducted in the West Midlands last year showed most Asians interviewed would welcome information from pharmacists in their own language.

The pharmacists especially liked the bottle leaflet which they thought innovative, eye-catching, and well designed – which contributed to its success; each pharmacy gave away about sixty copies. Its originality made it a conversation trigger but some customers thought some of the statements it made incredible. It seems people are not yet willing to believe some of the dangers associated with what they see as relatively low amounts of alcohol, and more publicity is needed. The most widely taken leaflet was on medicines and alcohol since the pharmacists could offer it with prescriptions without any embarrassment. This led to many questions on potential interactions between alcohol and medicines. It seems people are happy to openly ask questions about this issue although they are, understandably, unlikely to discuss more personal problems in a public pharmacy. Pharmacists were pleased with the project, more than one-third thinking it to be very useful, although they noted they could not initiate discussions about alcohol misuse in the same way as they volunteer advice to smokers. Local doctors saw the leaflets in some pharmacies and took a number away for surgery use.

The profile of pharmacy customers showed that, remarkably, 61 per cent of the women and 36 per cent of the men interviewed visit a pharmacy once a week or more, the most frequent users being women aged from 25 to 64. Nearly 20 per cent had seen the material, which was encouraging bearing in mind it was displayed for only three weeks. The majority, 143 (60 per cent), said they would seek help for alcohol problems from their doctor while only 16 per cent would ask for such help from the pharmacist – mainly citing the lack of privacy as the reason for not doing so.

The majority of women in all age groups said they would ask for help on health matters from their pharmacist and many had already done so – most often quoting upper respiratory tract infections, baby and child care, and the control of minor symptoms. None had asked for help on staying healthy, and pharmacists will have to promote this role if they wish to offer advice and guidance of this sort.

Most people knew it was dangerous to take alcohol with medicines but were less sure when to take special care, although guidance is given on the label which, when needed, bears a 'no alcohol' warning. Not many people could accurately identify the relative strengths of different types of alcoholic drinks. Could you? The only group where a majority knew a pint of beer was stronger than a single whisky were women aged 25 to 44. Perhaps the men had more difficulty accepting this fact. Most people interviewed drank alcohol but very few did so every day.

Conclusion

Any locality has a large number of pharmacies which could provide local prevention groups with an opportunity to disseminate alcohol education. Our project suggests that, providing the materials used are well designed, many of the surprisingly large numbers of people who regularly use pharmacies will find them useful and interesting. A full report on both the organization and findings of the project was produced and copies are available from Rhona Panton, Principal Pharmacist Education and Training, West Midlands RHA, Newland House, 139 Hagley Road, Birmingham, B16 8UA. The Report had three main conclusions. First, any future programme should employ self-assessment alcohol information leaflets in the main Indian languages in order to overcome the most important communication barrier the project encountered. These leaflets, funded by the RHA, are now being produced. Second, it recommended the production of a leaflet on medicines and alcohol which also incorporated straightforward material on sensible drinking, thus incorporating all the central messages into one piece of material. Such a leaflet could then be widely used in pharmacies and also in doctors' surgeries. Finally, the Report noted that work is needed to see if doctors want help in acquiring the knowledge and skills needed to take on a counselling role where alcohol-related problems are concerned.

Active consideration is currently being given in committee to the ways in which doctors can be helped to provide counselling on this subject. Clearly, a successful pharmacy-based alcohol education project can become the springboard for an on-going programme using these important outlets and also act as a catalyst, awakening interest in the subject, among other professional groups and organizations.

Note

This article first appeared in June 1987 as 'The risks and dangers of excess drinking: customers find out from pharmacists', in *Twenty Two*, Health News in the 22 Districts of the West Midlands, issue 10.

Pressing for prevention

Dr John G. Bligh

After attending the 34th International Conference on Drug and Alcohol Dependence in Calgary I realized the need for a group in my area to deal with alcohol problems. Chester and Ellesmere Port does not have a district alcohol service but is fortunate enough to have a regional unit for drug and alcohol dependence at the main psychiatric hospital in Chester at which I do two sessions a week as a clinical assistant. In 1985, in response to the DHSS guidelines to district health authorities concerning local action about drug (opiate) misuse, a District Drug Advisory Committee was set up by the district medical officer, and I was the general practice representative on that committee. The work of this committee was entirely directed towards improving facilities for the treatment of heroin misusers (although recently awareness of benzodiazepine misuse has widened its remit).

I used contacts made through this committee. I wrote to people who I thought would be interested in or sympathetic towards starting a separate group to consider what I described as 'the considerably more important and more insidious problem of alcohol misuse in our local area'. I was thus particularly well-placed to initiate appropriate contacts, but anyone thinking of setting up a local prevention group does not need ready-made links of this kind. Names and addresses of those whom you will want to reach will be readily available and many appropriate people can be contacted through mutual colleagues.

This initial letter proposed a meeting at my surgery to discuss the venture, and to talk over the implications of some facts and statistics about alcohol misuse, both national and local, that I had included in a briefing paper circulated with the letter. This paper included my estimates of some of the demands on the local hospital services given research findings that one in five admissions to hospital wards and 32 per cent of accident and emergency attenders have a significant alcohol problem. The paper also included some figures from the Chief Constable of Cheshire's report concerning arrests for simple drunkenness, drink-driving, and serving minors as well as figures from the local voluntary counselling agency's report showing local demand for help. I think it is very important that any initial approach to individuals, groups, and organizations to join a local prevention group should be accompanied by a briefing paper of this kind outlining the extent of the problem and the consequences for service providers of all kinds.

The first meeting was attended by representatives from the social services department, the probation service, our local health education department, general practice, clinical psychology, and the district health authority. Since then representatives of other organizations such as the police drug squad, the local education authority, and occupational nursing have also attended. Every locality will, I am sure, find representatives from these and other groups, eager to join a local prevention group that promises action and not just talk. Which organizations in your locality would you invite?

Meetings are now held monthly, and since our numbers have grown we have moved our venue to the local postgraduate centre, although we have also met in the local offices of the probation service and at the premises of Turning Point, the housing charity. We decided to call ourselves the Chester and Ellesmere Port Alcohol Forum with the aims of:

- identifying the extent of problems caused by alcohol misuse in the health district;
- identifying services and recognizing gaps;
- devising and encouraging the implementation of a community-based prevention strategy; and
- bringing together interested people representing as wide a range of services and professions as possible.

It soon became obvious that, with this remit, there was going to be a future to the group and lots of work to do, and we took steps to formalize our structure with the appointment of a chairperson, a secretary (for note-taking, circulation of notices, etc.), and a treasurer to cope with funds donated towards running costs by both the DHA and the local social services department.

Local issues under current consideration include 'alcohol and young people'. We are aware that local clubs have been making available books of admission tickets for parties and then not adequately supervising the sale of alcohol to those under eighteen. We are also trying to become involved with an initiative in Liverpool concerning the conversion of local pubs to provide alcohol-free entertainment for young people and to extend that initiative to our own area. We are also hoping to establish formal links with licensing magistrates to open a forum for discussion. Alcohol and work is another area of current interest and we were lucky enough to have a meeting with the county council medical officer and other occupational nursing staff to hear about their present workplace policy. Membership of the Forum is free and is open to anyone who has an interest in sharing the aims and the work of the group.

What have we achieved?

In October 1986 we organized and ran a workshop for local people involved in working with alcohol misusers. The meeting was entitled 'Practical Help for Problem Drinkers' and attracted over ninety participants from a wide range of backgrounds. They were organized in small groups led by local, experienced alcohol workers. The general aims included encouraging practical help for clients by allowing participants to examine their own attitudes to drinking and drinkers and to encourage communication between professional disciplines. The day also involved participants in taking a 'drinking history' from another group member and then discussing the feelings that this exercise created. More specifically, our Forum used the day to find out from participants what they thought of existing services and facilities and to see how they thought these could be improved. Brainstorming group work provided plenty of feedback. For example, one group looking into service needs identified gaps in treatment services including the lack of dry centres, family unit facilities, and local centres. In addition GPs' referral problems were highlighted as was the inadequate number of alcohol counsellors available for GPs' patients. Participants also identified problems with support services and pinpointed target areas for alcohol education such as schools, employers, and the Youth Service. Other local prevention groups might find that a similar kind of day will give them local credibility, widen their range of contacts, and identify an agenda for action. Certainly, our day ended with professional groups defining their agency response to the thoughts generated by the day and developing, at least in embryo, a plan for future action.

One of the points to emerge from the briefing paper that I had originally circulated was the implication that if 20 per cent of general medical admissions to hospital were alcohol related then over 800 people were passing through the medical wards of our local district general hospital every year with an alcohol problem. Furthermore, Hospital Activity Analysis figures (although notorious for their unreliability) suggested that only around 50 people per year were being diagnosed as having an alcohol-related problem. Personal contact was made with one of the local consultant physicians and the local consultant psychiatrist in charge of the Regional Dependence Unit and I presented a paper at one of the monthly clinical meetings of the medical unit at the hospital. The paper described how effective simple quantity/frequency questions and questionnaires (e.g. the CAGE) can be in detecting heavy drinkers in hospital. It also showed the usefulness of simple counselling about healthy drinking to in-patients. As a result, housemen on the medical wards now have greater knowledge and understanding of alcohol problems and their importance and, better still, ask effective questions about drinking when examining patients. A plan to repeat the paper each year has been agreed and the link with staff at the Regional Dependence Unit is being developed.

We have recently launched a newsletter, *Alcohol – News and Views,* with a circulation of 1,500. The initial cost of production was about £300, and we are grateful to CP Pharmaceuticals, the manufacturers of Antabuse, for their generous support of this edition. Funds for further quarterly editions are being (successfully) sought. The newsletter aims to be chatty, informative, up to date, and above all readable, and has received good reviews so far! The editorial work is shared by a team of three – we are learning the importance of sharing tasks!

What are the benefits of the Forum?

The Forum provides an opportunity for people with similar work interests and responsibilities to meet and exchange information. It helps to develop trust between therapists and agencies and enables them to talk face to face about matters of mutual interest and concern.

It is a form of community action group and, as such, has raised local awareness of the problems of alcohol misuse. This is achieved by liaison with the media, by the newsletter, and by the dissemination of ideas through discussion and the workshop which I have described.

The Forum is, thus, an educational instrument, not only for the public, professionals, and workers in the field with which it comes into contact, but also for its individual members. We have learnt about what others are doing in their jobs, what they would like to do, and about that which they cannot do because of financial or other limitations. We have exchanged ideas, improved inter-agency co-operation, and, most importantly, to some extent prevented duplication of effort. Keeping up to date in a developing field is difficult and the Forum has helped ease this process for many of us. The workshop was a splendid example of inter-agency co-operation.

The raising of local awareness of the problems of alcohol misuse increases the chance of alcohol-related services being seen as important, relevant, useful, and worthy of support. Local alcohol services have also benefited by an increase in their awareness of the facilities offered by others and have in some cases improved the expertise of their staff in working with problem drinkers.

The work of the Forum is regularly brought to the attention of the District Drugs Advisory Committee, the Joint Care Planning Team, the DHA, the social services, and the probation service. We have recently been closely involved with the development of the Chester Community Drug and Alcohol Team, which took up post in January 1987.

So what of the problems?

All members of the Forum (there are about nine regular members) are volunteers. They are also, as one would expect, heavily committed to their own jobs. The Forum started because of the initiative of one person but it very soon gained momentum by the addition of enthusiastic and active members. We are learning that the sharing of tasks such as the generation of agendas, the writing up and distribution of minutes, and supporting the treasurer at busy times are essential to maintain both motivation and enthusiasm. We have found that too great a reliance on one or two members of the group has led to over-burdening and to failure of continuity during periods of annual leave and sickness. The threat that work pressures and family life may lead to the Forum becoming simply a 'talking shop' rather than a group committed to action is acknowledged. Should we be looking for professional support on a sessional basis? Money, so far, because of our low running costs, has not been a real problem. The DHA and the local social services department have been very generous in their provision of support. This has been facilitated by personal contact with the chairman of the DHA.

If we could start again what would we change? Earlier diversification of tasks and improved contact between members is probably the most effective change that we could make. In the future, we will be looking to build up links with the drinks trade, the police (especially over road safety), and alcohol and workplace policy makers. We also hope to increase our involvement with professional skills training (a counselling course is planned). A priority for the future is the development of a local prevention strategy but we are wary of being seen as 'killjoys' or 'prohibitionists' in case we lose credibility, so we are treading carefully here. However, we have over the years come to a consensus view that 'sensible drinking' is:

not drinking and driving;
not drinking and working;
not drinking whilst pregnant; and
having two or three alcohol-free days every week.

You may decide on another set of statements around which to plan your activities. Your membership may be more or less than ours but however your prevention group is organized you will find much valuable work for it to do in bringing together different statutory and non-statutory workers of every kind to press for prevention.

Alcohol, the offender, and safety

Introduction

Alcohol is implicated in many different kinds of offence although the links between alcohol consumption and offending are complex. In many offending issues there is also a safety component. A number of local schemes and initiatives designed to tackle the alcohol and offender link preceded the Heysel stadium disaster in 1985. However, that single, tragic incident appears, in retrospect, a major turning point in the alcohol and crime debate. The climate of opinion has changed. Demands for action by politicians, the media, and the public became commonplace. The part that alcohol plays in hooliganism and the links between alcohol and other forms of offending assumed a higher profile. The subject of alcohol-related crime has become a regular newspaper topic and frequently appears as an agenda item at conferences. Those at the local level, who have long been voicing their concern about the issue, are now being asked for advice, comment, and, above all, plans for action. They are no longer regarded as being cranks or, at best, having 'a thing about drink'.

Many of the early alcohol and offending initiatives were based on the efforts of a few committed and convinced individuals. But the initiatives were often isolated and peripheral. Cautioning schemes run by police forces were small in number and patchy in distribution. The first national conference on drinking and driving did not take place until 1985. At that conference it was revealed that both national and local level organizations, such as road safety departments, the police, and the Department of Transport, were not only going their separate ways, but giving contradictory messages. However, it is clear from the six case studies in this section that things are changing. Not only are the efforts of the pioneers being recognized but collaboration between different groups and organizations is now seen as vital.

The authors of the case studies come from both statutory and non-statutory services. All have extensive professional experience and none doubt that alcohol and offending are intimately related. Two of the authors are probation officers, which is not surprising considering that their service has been at the forefront of innovative local schemes designed to identify offenders with alcohol problems and to help them overcome their difficulties. Jeanne Wesson's description of the beginnings of the Aquarius Court Alcohol Service in

Birmingham and its subsequent development emphasizes the key role which the probation service has played. She takes us to the heart of how the all-important organizational collaboration is actually achieved and highlights the difficult and delicate negotiations which are necessary if an innovative local project of this kind is to become accepted by the professional groups within the criminal justice system. She reminds us that although there is now much wider recognition of the importance of alcohol and offender initiatives, energy and commitment is still needed to enthuse those who have other time-consuming responsibilities. Informal talks and telephone calls proved as important as minuted meetings in preparing the ground and convincing doubtful professionals of the need for the kind of service which was proposed. Her account is full of tips on how to accommodate oneself to the ideals and practices of other groups without sacrificing one's own objectives.

The Aquarius Court Alcohol Service has, in a very few years, proved itself to magistrates and other cautious professional groups as a viable and valuable service. It is undoubtedly a model for other localities and emulators might like to take careful note of the way in which the developing service acquired hard data on the numbers of alcohol-related offenders going through the system and took steps to publicize the range of disposal options available to magistrates. The increased range of options available to offenders and court professionals emphasize the value of developing clear objectives and sound partnerships.

Setting clear objectives is important in any local initiative. This is as true for education groups for alcohol offenders as for other schemes. Such groups are spreading. The Aquarius Alcohol Court Service has helped to set them up in Birmingham. David Taylor provides an account of their development in Hull. As his case study makes clear, it is not only groups within the criminal justice system which have to be persuaded of the need to develop strategies of this kind. Frequently, one's own professional colleagues must be convinced too. Given the numbers of offenders with alcohol problems of various kinds, it is clearly in everyone's interest to identify and help those in difficulties. But, until local research is available to convince the doubters, short-term considerations will continue to be an impediment to local action. Taylor emphasizes the importance of carefully targeting the kinds of offenders whom the groups are designed to help in order to allay fears of over-stretching resources and to clarify aims and working methods.

David Taylor takes us carefully through the planning processes and emphasizes the value of monitoring progress through sound data collection. He is honest enough to highlight the fact that, in spite of all this planning and thought, problems still remained. His comments on the general failure of magistrates to make use of the alcohol education group alternative when probation officers are not in court are particularly interesting. As he says, this failure may be due to a lack of 'alcohol awareness' on the part of many magistrates which points up the need for more and better alcohol education in their formal training programmes. Emulators in other areas might find it helpful to consider whether their local Bench training programme would benefit from the inclusion of an alcohol education component.

Anyone operating on the assumption that a successful scheme developed in one area only has to be taken off the shelf and imported into another will learn much from John Cook's account of the development of the course for alcohol-impaired drivers in Hampshire. This is probably one of the best known innovations among probation officers and workers in the alcohol field. John Cook and his colleagues have done much to assist those wanting to develop discussions at the local level about how best to divert drinking drivers towards educational responses. Even so, such discussions do not simply happen by walking into a meeting after posting the Hampshire manual to local magistrates. The same pattern of planning, persuading, and influencing local key people is vital. Getting prevention initiatives accepted in local political and professional structures is time-consuming and labour intensive. Moreover, one has only to read this account of course content to realize that whilst much of the basic work has been done for us considerable effort is needed to re-fashion educational materials and approaches and adapt them to particular local circumstances and aims.

Cook emphasizes that education groups for drinking drivers have a specialist function and that the inclusion of other kinds of offender is unhelpful. This is confirmed by the Taylor and Wesson case studies. In Hull, drinking drivers are excluded from alcohol education groups. In Birmingham, drinking drivers have their own groups. An important feature of the groups in Hampshire is that all drivers convicted of being over the legal limit qualify for attendance. Unfortunately, it is still widely believed that the only indication of a drink problem is high blood/alcohol concentration at arrest. This is not true and problem drinkers are distributed throughout the whole range of blood/alcohol levels (Dunbar *et al.*, 1985: 827–30).

John Cook's account also emphasizes the importance of good media relationships and the right kind of publicity in getting an idea across not only to professional groups but also to the general public. However, even though Cook had helpful publicity early in the history of his proposal it did not obviate the need to personally persuade and convince the same groups in the criminal justice system which other contributors in this section had to convince. The case study confirms David Taylor's assertion that offenders find this kind of initiative interesting and convincing. John Cook has helped to produce a teaching pack to disseminate the lessons learned in Hampshire. Given the toll of death and injury on our roads it is difficult to understand why every locality does not have a course for impaired drivers on the Hampshire lines. This is an urgent question which readers might like to ask of their local Bench, road safety department, probation committee, and council on alcoholism.

Much of the relationship between alcohol and offending has a safety dimension, whether that is as part of public disorder, violent death, or road accidents. In many of these cases the coroner becomes involved. Dr Richard

Whittington outlines the coroner's duty to investigate violent, sudden, or unnatural deaths, highlights the role of alcohol, and draws attention to the attendant risks of drinking in hazardous circumstances. Before action at a local or national level is possible a raised level of public concern is often vital. This point is taken up by John Knight, one of the founder members of the Campaign Against Drinking and Driving (CADD), who discusses the question of how to start raising public awareness. As he says:

> So you have an issue which you feel needs addressing, or perhaps there is an aspect of life which you feel is harmful and could be improved, or is downright wrong and something should be done about it. What can you do?

Knight's account of the steps he and his colleagues took to establish CADD as a major national force in the area of drinking and driving is full of information, tips, and advice. In fact it could sit easily in any book written about pressure group activity in any field. It is particularly pertinent to have it in this section of this book because those involved with and concerned about aspects of alcohol and safety which have not reached the attention of the public can take comfort from the fact that CADD was two people and an idea in 1985. The careful, detailed advice backed by the commitment of a few people can, as John Knight demonstrates, achieve a great deal. Legislative change is on the way, accident rates are falling, and a new healthy awareness about drinking and driving is reflected in many parts of the country. CADD has played a part in this.

The final contribution comes from Mike McKnight, the Principal Engineer of the Road Safety Unit of the City of Birmingham. Within the text of his account of work related to drinking and driving in Birmingham emerges the value of bringing together apparently unconnected organizations: police, health education, city engineers, licensed victuallers, and more. Through a combination of crossing organizational boundaries and involving people who are not precious about their own territory, action is possible.

The initiatives described in these case studies were all built, and continue to survive, on commitment, sound argument based on good data collection, careful planning, and sound inter-organizational relationships. In a number of cases, the success can be very much attributed to a recognition of the importance of local political and professional structures. All the case studies emphasize just how much can be done at the local level by those who can both credibly demonstrate the extent of local problems and persuade other groups and organizations to share their concerns. Their success has altered the questions that should be asked. It is now not just a case of 'Should we have a court alcohol worker and try to develop alcohol education initiatives for offenders?', but 'Why haven't we developed ways of identifying offenders with alcohol problems who can then be helped?' These are questions that must be asked in every locality which lacks a coherent strategy in relation to alcohol, the offender, and safety.

Reference

Dunbar, J.A., Simon, A.O., Ritchie, A., Devgun, M.S., Hagart, J., and Martin, B.T. (1985) 'Are problem drinkers dangerous drivers?', *British Medical Journal* 290: 827–30.

The Aquarius Court Alcohol Service

Jeanne Wesson

The Aquarius Court Alcohol Service, currently situated on the first floor of the Victoria Law Courts in Birmingham, was conceived by workers who, in one way or another, had regular contact with or responsibility for drunken offenders or those whose offences were drink-related. They felt frustrated at not being able to respond helpfully when such offenders appeared in court. The probation service in Birmingham was committed to alternatives to custodial sentencing and felt there should be more intervention in such cases even though the Homeless Alcohol Recovery Project (HARP), a non-statutory initiative developed by a probation officer, had begun to offer an important 'drop-in' service. Aquarius, established for a decade, had up to that point concentrated almost entirely on providing accommodation for those suffering from a range of alcohol-related problems and providing a personal skills training approach to recovery. However, it too recognized that a different response was needed if an adequate approach to problem drinkers at a time of personal crisis was to be developed.

Workers in both these organizations knew that there were large, but at that time unquantified, numbers of individuals passing through the Victoria Law Courts who had drinking problems and whose offences were clearly drink-related, but in whom the alcohol component went entirely unnoticed and, therefore, un-responded to. They saw the same men and women revolving through the courts without any attention being paid to their drinking record or drink-related behaviour. Such a spectacle was frustrating since, as Aquarius's experience shows, even minimal intervention can improve an individual's quality of life and the possibility of reoffending, thus saving the taxpayers' money and the courts' time.

The planning

New schemes mean workers, plant, financing, and organizational commitment. Discussions and negotiations took place on the idea of developing a court alcohol service but these were inevitably slow since the individuals involved already had time-consuming management responsibilities. In retrospect, as with most development projects, it is difficult to know who first spoke to whom. Perceptions of the ownership of ideas and initiatives are frequently as varied as the number of people involved. Suffice to say that the negotiations, which ranged from informal chats and telephone calls to more formal minuted occasions, took place chiefly between one of the assistant chief probation officers, a senior probation officer, the Clerk to the Justices, and the director of Aquarius. The core idea was to provide, within the Victoria Law Courts, a worker whose sole responsibility would be to concentrate on helping to identify defendants whose drinking and offending were linked and who would assist the criminal justice system to deal more effectively with the alcohol aspects of drink-related offending.

To finance the proposed project, Aquarius turned to the Barrow and Geraldine S. Cadbury Trust which had supported it during its formative years. The Trustees were happy to help develop a court alcohol service of the type proposed which they felt would be able to intervene where help was most needed and affect key policy changes.

The service

The job description of the court alcohol worker was formidable but, fortunately for all concerned, we were lucky enough to find someone with the necessary knowledge, energy, and commitment capable of handling the innovatory tasks involved. As the worker at HARP, Nicky James had already established good working relationships with the probation service and had the necessary experience of liaising with relevant agencies.

The Aquarius Court Alcohol Service began in April 1984 in a small room at the Victoria Law Courts. The newly-appointed Court Alcohol Worker liaised in her day-to-day activities with the probation service and the Clerk to the Justices although she was ultimately responsible to Aquarius. The Court Alcohol Service has a clearly defined task which is to encourage, tickle, and prod the criminal justice system to deal more effectively with alcohol aspects of drink-related offending. This is no easy job since, as those close to it know, the criminal justice system encompasses not merely structures but many different groups of people including judges, magistrates, court clerks, probation officers, and the police, all with their own ways of working, their own training, their own professional organizations, hierarchies, communication systems, and, more subtle still, their own cultures and ways of thinking. What is more, they have well established ways of negotiating with one another. Finally, there is the defendant.

A court alcohol service needs to establish good working relationships with all these people inside the complex criminal justice system, generate and collect information on alcohol offending, and devise appropriate intervention services. You need a development worker who can cope with a variety of tasks and seize every opportunity to advance on a number of fronts. By June 1985, the

Service had assembled telling data which showed that 40–70 per cent of imprisoned offenders were intoxicated at the time of their offence and that 9 per cent of the daily lock-up list included alcohol offences. This was quite apart from the 1,900 annual drink-driving disqualifications. Here was the beginning of some factual and local evidence of the type which impresses and convinces workers in other organizations and the media that a serious problem exists. The data were widely publicized by the Court Alcohol Service in a leaflet distributed to all court personnel.

Much of the information was collected by means of a questionnaire designed by the Court Alcohol Service but administered by probation officers at the end of Social Enquiry Report (SER) interviews. In five probation offices 322 questionnaires were completed and these indicated that one-third of clients had a drink problem. This conclusion was reached on the basis of defendants' evaluation of themselves together with the probation officers' assessments. The implications of this finding are far-reaching and confirm the need to establish early identification procedures in courts and to develop more widespread use of early intervention techniques.

The Service had an almost immediate impact. Shortly after its inception, magistrates were beginning to recommend that some defendants with drink offences should either visit the Court Alcohol Service or were asking for the Alcohol Service Worker to be called to the court. Verbal opinions and written reports were being presented by the Service to magistrates. Concerned families were seen on request and enquiries were also beginning to come in by telephone. The Probation Alcohol Group distributed a card to magistrates outlining the options for positive non-custodial sentences for alcohol-related offences. By this time, these included alcohol education groups for defendants who are at risk of a custodial sentence. Defendants must be prepared to accept a Probation Order subject to the additional clause 'Shall attend in a sober condition six consecutive weekly sessions of an Alcohol Education Group, as directed by the Probation Officer'. The aim of these groups is to increase defendants' knowledge of alcohol, give them some understanding of their own alcohol behaviour, and teach them some methods and skills for personal problem solving. The Aquarius Court Alcohol Service shares responsibility for running these groups with the probation service.

The drink-driving issue provided a platform for further Court Alcohol Service development. Building on the concept of the alcohol education groups, plans for a specific education project for those with drink-drive offences were developed. A joint probation service and Court Alcohol Service application to fund an initiative in this area was submitted for Inner-City Partnership funding but unfortunately it failed as did a subsequent application to the Brewers. Anyone hoping to do innovative work in this kind of area must be prepared for disappointments. However, the time was not entirely wasted since important relationships with such organizations as the Royal Society for the Prevention of Accidents (RoSPA), Birmingham's Road Safety Unit, and the police were being established. Moreover, a watchful eye was being kept on the pioneering scheme for drink-drive education groups being developed by the Hampshire Probation Service (see John Cook's article). However, after a further round of fund-raising applications, sufficient money was received from a variety of local and national sources to launch a trial project for one year.

It was apparent that the Court Alcohol Service Worker could not carry the burden of the new initiative on her own even though she was now supported by an MSC-funded assistant and part-time secretarial help. Eventually, two workers were appointed to share the tasks on part-time contracts.

The Court Alcohol and Road Safety Course (CARS), the content of which has been devised by the Court Alcohol Service, is an alternative to imprisonment for recurrent drink-driving offenders appearing before Birmingham magistrates. The course is for second- and third-time offenders. They are required not to have a history of other offences. Defendants must be prepared to accept a Probation Order subject to the additional condition 'Shall attend in a sober condition, seven weekly sessions of a Court Alcohol and Road Safety Course as directed by the Probation Officer'. The aims of the course are to motivate individuals to separate their drinking and driving and to provide them with accurate information on the topic. By January 1988, twenty-one motorists had passed through the course and none had re-offended since attending.

By the end of 1986, the Court Alcohol Service was regularly providing an information and referral service for magistrates and helping to provide alcohol education for many different kinds of offender. However, it was also active in many other areas and any alcohol court service will find much to do. In Birmingham, the Service provides alcohol assessments for SERs and Stand Down Reports. It also monitors offenders with more than two named alcohol offences. The Service helped to establish a Probation Alcohol Group, assisted in training sessions for those involved in the courts, and helped to plan a major conference on drinking and driving which was part-funded by the city. As a result of these activities it has had to move to more appropriate accommodation within the Victoria Law Courts.

By the summer of 1987 a new Court Alcohol Service Worker had been appointed to replace the original development worker who had left to further her career and the third one-year MSC assistant was in post. One of the part-time drink-drive workers left on the completion of the year's appointment but the other has been retained to develop the Court Alcohol and Road Safety Course for a further three years. Funding to continue the Course has recently been obtained but, at the time of writing, finance is still being sought to enable the Court Alcohol Service to continue for a further period and expand its current programme of work. If all goes well, plans are afoot to develop work with younger drink-related offenders via the Court Alcohol Service and to develop a range of innovative drink-drive educational schemes and preventative activities of a voluntary nature with drivers and riders, involving inter-agency collaboration via Aquarius and its own Drink-Drive Project.

In the light of experience

Whilst we have goals, we do not always know exactly how we will reach them. We are committed to doing whatever we do well and to coping with the inevitable setbacks with support from colleagues and that essential commodity for development work of this kind, a sense of humour.

Our experience in the Court Alcohol Service team would suggest that whilst standards and training are necessary, skilled and experienced leadership is also essential for this type of development, so that the confidence of related services, agencies, and professions is maintained and developed. Research, designed to demonstrate the extent of alcohol-related problems and promote the credibility of proposals for a court alcohol service of the kind developed in Birmingham, are essential. Facts and figures must be collected to show why such a service is necessary and why many different professions and groups should take its claims seriously. The qualities of key workers are important. Adaptability is essential. The ability to seize opportunities and promote initiatives within goal-orientated boundaries and the perseverance to cope with organizational setbacks and funding problems is necessary. Key workers must have energy and commitment but also the diplomacy to deal with many different groups and sensitive organizational relationships. This highlights the need for supportive supervisory arrangements. Moreover, Birmingham's Aquarius Court Alcohol Service has sought to develop within the context of a vacillating stance by the Home Office towards alcohol-related offences and the Department of Transport on drink-driving counter measures.

An ability to withstand the prevailing political winds and sail with facts, figures, and maps of one's own seems necessary if a service of this kind is to maintain its momentum. Like Birmingham, the courts in your area will be routinely processing, every day of the week, offenders with drinking problems who ought to be helped. Do you know how many such offenders there are going through the local courts? Has any research on this question been carried out in your area? Are any steps being taken to identify such offenders and provide the minimal intervention which, experience now shows, can be successful in reducing re-offending? If there are no such initiatives, could you help to set the organizational ball rolling?

Alcohol problem groups in the probation service

David Taylor

The Alcohol Problem Groups run by the Humberside Probation Service were started in Hull in 1985. They were one of a range of initiatives forming part of a DHSS-funded project at Hull and York Universities. This involved the Accident and Emergency Department of the Hull Royal Infirmary, the Humberside Social Services Department, and the Humberside Probation Service. The aim of the project was to identify the extent of the alcohol component of the problems that are routinely dealt with by these three statutory services, to establish the cost of this component, and to explore what can be done to improve the recognition and management of alcohol problems. Thus, it was a piece of action research designed to promote service development. A report of the project entitled 'Problem Drinkers and the Statutory Services' was completed in 1986 and the volume dealing with the probation service is available on request from me at the Humberside Probation Service, 75 Goodhart Road, Hull, North Humberside, HU7 4EF.

For the probation service component of the project the research team together with Hull probation officers felt they and service managers formed the Project Planning Group and it was this group which identified the development of alcohol-problem groups, referred to in Hull as Alcohol Information and Assessment Groups, as being an important response for offenders with alcohol-related problems. The Service was receptive to such a proposal. A survey undertaken by the Service's Alcohol Abuse Standing Committee revealed that local probation officers felt they had a responsibility to help clients with a drink problem and that they believed the Service response to alcohol-related problems among clients should improve.

Local magistrates were concerned that something more should be done to help people with drink problems. This attitude was reinforced by a survey also undertaken in 1985 which sought to measure the extent of alcohol problems among clients over 80 per cent of whom are under 35 and more than 60 per cent are in the age range 17 to 25. Using the CAGE questionnaire, the survey revealed that 33 per cent were problem drinkers and that 25 per cent displayed medium to high dependence. There was a high degree of association between drinking and clients' offences in 26 per cent of the sample and only one offender in the sample of 273 had a current offence which was 'alcohol specific' and related either to pedestrian drunkenness or drunken driving. It seemed therefore both appropriate and timely that the Probation Service in Humberside should take an initiative which provided a new method of helping offenders and which encouraged magistrates to respond to information indicating that an offence may be alcohol-related.

The groups

The aim of the groups was to offer help to offenders who were at an early stage of a problematic drinking career and who would be most unlikely to seek help voluntarily. It was also seen as essential that magistrates should be involved in the selection process. Participation in a group should be another disposal option for magistrates and an alternative to custody. The target group was defined quite narrowly to allay fears that resources would be overstretched. They were designed primarily for 'early-stage' problem drinkers.

Magistrates were invited to remand for assessment any offender where it was thought that alcohol abuse may have led to the commission of an offence. Those with three or more convictions for drunkenness and drinking drivers were excluded. Probation staff would assess referrals and examine for evidence of alcohol-related problems, attitudes to drinking, suitability for a group, and willingness to be placed on probation for six months with the requirement 'to attend six consecutive group sessions in a sober condition'. Another route to the groups was through the inclusion of an 'alcohol requirement' in a Probation Order of any length following a recommendation and a Social Enquiry Report (SER) prepared by probation officers. The aim of the groups was to modify inappropriate, unhelpful, or unwise drinking behaviour through the provision of information about alcohol problems and the development of personal skills.

The Planning Group was responsible for designing the structure, working methods, and programme for the proposed groups. They were helped in this by the experience of other services running alcohol education groups. These groups, of which it was felt the Coventry experience offered a particularly helpful example, had emphasized that drinking is a learned behaviour and combined an educational component with social skills training designed to help clients deal with personal problem solving. It was decided to use the Coventry model although group leaders would modify it as appropriate in order to meet particular client needs.

At the inception of the DHSS project it was understood that there would be no significant increase in resources to support the Service after the end of the project. The aim was to try to improve officers' response to the alcohol problems they were already encountering and to focus their work on those areas of client behaviour where change was needed if criminal activity was to be avoided. It is important, therefore, to increase officer awareness of alcohol problems and to develop existing skills to tackle them.

Despite their overall supportive attitude revealed in the early survey, the interest and support of officers for the project became problematical and a principal concern for the Planning Group. This was a direct result of the increasing burdens being placed upon officers in their general work load and the fact that monitoring and data collection required by the project were felt to be a heavy imposition. Worries were beginning to be expressed that in setting up the groups, the Service might be taking on a different client group for which resources did not exist. The interest and attitudes of probation officers when the groups started were mixed. Some were interested, enthusiastic, and wholly committed. Others, after a prolonged planning period, were either being diverted away by other service activities or were losing interest. Fortunately, sufficient commitment existed for a small group of staff to run the groups for at least one year at a rate of one group every two months. Despite the difficulties outlined, the general level of awareness of officers within the Service through discussion, provision of literature, and 'awareness days' was satisfactory.

Contacting and persuading the 150 magistrates in the Service area was difficult. As in most probation areas, the Humberside Service has close contact with about 20 per cent of local Justices through probation liaison committees. About sixty magistrates, together with their clerks, attended a launching/preparation event and clearly seemed to welcome the initiative. Within a short period of the commencement date, the flow of referrals increased and before very long was sufficient to fully utilize the staff resources for the running of the groups. Each group had two leaders – either two probation officers or a probation officer and a probation service assistant. A voluntary worker was also used. He or she was a member of the first group who had found it very helpful and who was skilled in imparting confidence to members of later groups, thus enabling them to talk about their experiences and share their feelings. Towards the end of 1985, the groups had become an accepted part of local probation practice and gradually it seemed that the initial reservations held by some officers about compulsory attendance at groups were being dissolved. This is probably attributable to the fact that every effort was made to ensure feedback to officers about progress of the groups.

The invitation to magistrates to remand offenders for short periods on the day of the court hearing for assessment was never really taken up. The reason for this is not entirely clear. It may be that it was an unrealistic expectation on the Probation Service's part that magistrates would be able to spot signs of possible drink abuse without the sort of preparation given to probation officers. There was some indication that with the pressures on local courts, there was reluctance to hold things up whilst the Probation Service made explorations. However, there was plenty of evidence that when the Service, through its personnel in court, were ready to prompt, magistrates would accept the lead. The view was also expressed that the package presented to magistrates was not sufficiently attractive and credible as an alternative to custody when the offender had committed a serious offence. Six sessions with an alcohol problem group did not seem to be 'heavy enough' compared with, say, the sixty day attendance of a day centre requirement.

During the early weeks of running the groups there was difficulty obtaining a sufficient flow of clients. It was important to work to a minimum group size of six, and to achieve that it occasionally meant that some offenders were waiting several weeks before their groups started with the attendant risk of a further offence occurring before any help had been given. However, by the end of the first year the flow of clients was far more satisfactory, but problems then began to emerge about staffing and sustaining the impetus once the DHSS Project was complete. Resolving these difficulties took many months.

The selection process proved to be effective in producing target group clients who had been drinking immediately prior to committing their offences and who themselves saw a link between the consumption of alcohol and their offending. In a questionnaire completed by members of a group commencing in May 1986 clients saw a number of links between their offence and alcohol. These included 'Because I was drunk and normally wouldn't do it', 'It made me mad', and 'Dutch courage makes you feel you don't care'. A copy of this questionnaire is available from me at the address given earlier. None of these clients had sought any advice or help to manage their drinking but all thought drink had played a part in previous offences. In this particular group, six out of seven saw themselves as people whose drinking often leads to problems either for themselves or their families, and two identified physical problems resulting from drinking. When asked what changes they would like to see in their drinking habits, they gave a number of answers including 'I would like to drink less', 'Not be so violent', and 'To drink less when I go out'.

Generally, the style of the groups was found to be satisfactory to the clients. The atmosphere was described by them as being relaxed, friendly, and interesting. Most fairly rapidly came to terms with the compulsory attendance aspect and found their involvement as a 'student' on the course quite acceptable. Motivating the group was critically important but members, having arrived, could choose to either participate or opt out. Approximately 50 per cent of group members managed to control their drinking better and actually cut down the amount they consumed. The majority seemed to have been able to use the groups to advantage.

Staff running the groups found them very challenging. Experience of working with groups of young people was important as was the confidence gained from being well prepared and familiar with background literature on alcohol education groups in general and the Coventry experience in particular. Most leaders found that it was necessary to be flexible in the use of the material and that it was necessary to give plenty of space during the sessions for working with individual members. The literacy level of some members made it difficult for them to stay the course.

Resources did not allow for follow-up studies and, therefore, views about the effectiveness of the groups were derived from assessing increase in knowledge, reported modification of drinking practice and consumption levels, and whether the clients themselves believed that the course had been worthwhile and that it had led to significant changes. Results lead us to believe that the groups must be regarded as a credible and important new response to some offenders with alcohol-related problems.

Service development

The difficulties experienced in establishing the groups were characteristic of those met in the DHSS Project as a whole. They brought into focus important issues which need to be addressed when seeking to advance probation practice throughout the area.

Setting up groups by way of capitalizing on the interest and commitment of a few officers (an innovation, piloting a new method of practice) is a very different exercise from that of achieving the broader aims described in the early part of this paper where the primary objective was to improve overall the Service response to drink problems – the groups offering an additional method of helping. In the former, a successful outcome requires the ownership of the initiative by the few enthusiasts, preparation, authority to proceed, and space to engage, whereas with the latter all officers serving a large urban area were to participate, requiring a level of practice management not experienced hitherto.

The project contributed substantially to a growing debate about achieving change within the Service and, in particular, management effectiveness. In 1982, when the project was being negotiated, the methods of obtaining the participation of the Hull teams (informing, negotiating with teams individually, agreement to support) proved wholly inadequate – the management 'culture' simply did not meet the needs. Today, the process would be tackled differently: once the Service had made a commitment to such an exercise, the programme of activities would be secured through the setting of Hull area and team objectives with the resource implications being addressed by management as a whole. With the Probation Service at Hull finding difficulties building upon the interest expressed in improving its work with drinkers, it is perhaps not surprising that achieving significant change in the response of magistrates and court clerks was less than successful. Publicizing proposals through literature and addressing meetings was clearly insufficient, even as a start. Subsequent experience has shown that the way forward in the court arena lies more with a proactive Probation presence day-to-day at court – officers who are alert to indications of alcohol problems before and during hearings and who are able to take initiatives to assist magistrates in their sentencing task. A specialist court team has now been created at Hull. Additionally, the task of keeping magistrates up-to-date on developments is a long-term exercise requiring frequent and varied presentations. Each time a Social Enquiry Report recommends attendance at a group, it should be accompanied with an appropriate information sheet.

The probation component of the DHSS Project was about service development – developing officers' practice. Three years on, as the calls for the Service to demonstrate its effectiveness grow stronger, the management of change comes increasingly under review. The elements of the Project designed to increase officers' interest and awareness, develop skills and practice aids, were all-important. With hindsight it can be seen that even with the endorsement of the Service management, change does not necessarily emerge. Without management's full participation exercising their critical roles (objective setting, monitoring, rewards, identifying responsibilities), the ability to lift performance is seriously handicapped and allows the business of responding to alcohol-related problems to remain a marginalized activity.

A course for alcohol-impaired drivers

John Cook

The Road Safety Act, 1967, which introduced the 'breathalyser', had a considerable impact on the numbers of fatalities and injuries due to drink-drivers. However, the impact of this Act rapidly faded and drink-drivers have been appearing before the courts in steadily increasing numbers. Offenders have been dealt with by the imposition of fines, mandatory disqualification, and, increasingly, imprisonment. The courts have thus had few sentencing options from which to choose and none of the options available encouraged or enabled offenders to examine their attitudes and behaviour in relation to the use of alcohol or to make the connection between alcohol and the deterioration of driving skills and abilities.

In March 1983, my increasing concern at seeing drink-drivers leaving the courts little wiser for the experience, and no better equipped to avoid repeat offences of this kind, led me to submit to my Service a proposal for an alcohol education programme specifically focused on the drink-driver. I suggested that an appropriate alcohol education course should be designed and that attendance on such a course for drink-drivers should be made a condition, if they agreed, of a Probation Order. The response was immediate and positive, in marked contrast to the lukewarm and largely negative response from my own team.

I originally proposed the Blood Alcohol Concentration (BAC) criterion for inclusion in the kind of scheme I envisaged should be set at the legal blood/alcohol limit for drivers which is 80 mg/100 ml. However, after lengthy argument with my colleagues I backed down, agreeing to 2½ times the legal limit, i.e. 200 mg/100 ml. This level is the main ground on which drivers qualify for inclusion in the national High Risk Offender scheme. Under this scheme, offenders have their licences withdrawn and they are not returned until the authorities are convinced that any drinking problem is under control. It is designed to identify problem drinkers and remove them from the roads until they have demonstrated they are capable of driving safely once again. However, this scheme is totally inadequate since research has shown that blood/alcohol concentration is no guide to chronic impairment and drivers whose overall ability has deteriorated due to excessive drinking are found at all blood/alcohol levels.

When the proposal was discussed by the county probation committee, a judge firmly rejected such a high threshold on the basis that at that level he would be considering a sentence of imprisonment without option. I was asked to reconsider and suggest a compromise figure, but declined. I returned to my original argument that the threshold should be no more than the legal limit itself. To set a level above the legal limit would suggest that it was somehow acceptable to exceed it. In the event, qualification for inclusion on the drink-driving course was set at the legal limit.

It was essential to sell the idea to magistrates in my own court area and I was grateful to the Clerk to the Justices who allowed me to address them at their Annual General Meeting. Reaction was mixed and I felt that I probably carried about half the Bench with me at that time. I would now put the percentage in favour of the course as being in the region of 85 per cent or more. I also called a meeting of solicitors practising in the areas and the response from them was very positive, which is not surprising since the proposal offered a constructive alternative to existing penalties. Finally, I took the opportunity of sharing the idea with our local newspaper. Their court reporter produced an article which was most supportive, emphasizing the positive and constructive elements of the proposed course and the protection for the community which a successful outcome offered. It was a good example of responsible reporting and gave me some valuable experience in dealing with the media.

The first course started in August 1983 with the assistance of my colleague Rosemary Cole and the co-operation of a variety of outside speakers, which included a chief inspector of police, a consultant psychiatrist from an alcohol treatment unit, a member of Alcoholics Anonymous, a solicitor, and a senior counsellor from the Hampshire Council on Alcoholism. Having set up the course and advertised it to my colleagues, magistrates, and solicitors, it was essential to start quickly and not to defer it until we had some imaginary ideal number. Since we had insufficient drink-driving referrals, I added to the course existing clients of the Service whose offending was clearly alcohol-related. The two groups have not mixed particularly well and subsequent experience suggests that it is strongly desirable to restrict membership of such a course to drinking drivers.

The innovative nature of the course attracted the interest of Professor Martin of the University of Southampton, a co-opted member of the probation committee. He felt the course offered an opportunity for a mature student to research a Master's Degree. Mrs Terri Lawrence agreed to participate as a researcher/observer and was closely involved in the course. Her interest continued, following her formal employment by the Service as a County Research and Information Officer, until she left in September 1985 to take up appointment as Training and Development Officer for the National Association for the Care and Resettlement of Offenders (NACRO) in Birmingham. Her association with the course, her observations, and her own extensive knowledge in the field of alcohol education all contributed greatly to its development.

In Autumn 1984 a colleague, Mrs Katherine Jeary, a German-speaking probation officer, was commissioned by the Service to visit West Germany for a month in order to investigate the courses for alcohol-impaired drivers available in that country. On her return a formal review of the programme took place and headquarters allowed a month's leave of absence for Terri Lawrence, Katherine Jeary, Rosemary Cole, and myself to pursue the development of the course. The major change that emerged from this review was the switch away from invited speakers. Early experience suggested that this format was not helpful and did little to encourage group unity. Course leaders now undertake all aspects of course presentation. Feedback from course members was positive and confirmed the wisdom of the change.

Course structure and content

The course comprises eight two-hour sessions one evening each week. Course members are encouraged to bring with them one other person who can be either a friend or a relative. This policy pays clear dividends since, of the 30 per cent who are accompanied, the majority choose to bring along a regular drinking partner. The effect of this is to enable the course member to continue to discuss outside the course issues which were raised during the sessions and often to find support in resolutions for behavioural change.

The first session of the course sets the scene and re-emphasizes the consequences of failing to co-operate, which means a return to court to be sentenced for the original offence. It sets out to demonstrate by way of a variety of exercises the relative strengths of different alcoholic drinks and to show how easy it is to drink more than is intended. Information is also given on the speed at which alcohol is absorbed into the blood stream and how long it remains there before being broken down by the body. This underlines the dangers of driving to work hours later or even the next morning when motorists can still be above the legal limit. The second session examines the body's response to alcohol in general, and the third emphasizes the connection between alcohol and the deterioration in driving skills. A 20-minute scientific video film demonstrates the effects of drinking alcohol, even at levels below the legal threshold.

The fourth session is a role-play based on a typical drink-driving conviction. Magistrates, the Clerk to the Justices, crown prosecutors, solicitors, and the police join the course and help to enact a mock court scene in which the court officials lead discussions about their roles and responsibilities and the attitudes which they represent. Court members themselves are required to play the role of court officials and to sentence, taking into account the circumstances of the defendant and the attitudes of society. This is always the most popular session.

The fifth session focuses on the pattern of drinking and the difficulties of trying to break drinking habits which have been established over long periods. Role-play is used in the sixth session to help participants practise face-saving strategies in difficult drinking situations and these are introduced by a number of short trigger video films. A drinking diary is the focus of the seventh session and course members are required to give information about their drinking habits which is collated and related to the Health Education Authority (HEA) guidance on safe and sensible drinking levels.

During the last session, members are required to set themselves achievable goals for the future. Invariably, their primary goal is not to drink and drive at all. Other goals usually include resolutions to change their pattern of drinking in order to reduce overall consumption of alcohol and to seek alternative interests to fill the gap left by changes in behaviour. They were all given information about local agencies specializing in alcohol advice and support in order that those who wish to take further steps to combat problem drinking may do so.

During the course, each member is required to undergo publicly an offence examination. This is a re-living of their drink-driving offence and their behaviour during the course of that day and the previous evening. By correlating the amount of alcohol consumed and the number of hours over which drinking took place up until the time of the intoximeter readout, it is possible to check whether the course members are being truthful, or if there are indications of physical damage due to alcohol abuse. This also provides an opportunity to consider, with the benefit of hindsight, alternative behaviours which could have been adopted. Between sessions, course members are required to complete projects designed to reinforce lessons learned at the previous sessions or to prepare for the forthcoming one.

Initially, courses usually had a break of four weeks before referrals built up for the next course but increase in the number of referrals has led to the present situation where two courses are usually running at any one time. Interest in the course grew because of regular reports from the chief probation officer to the county probation committee on which all local Benches are represented. I have now attended ten meetings of magistrates in adjacent court areas which also now make referrals. Originally, the course was based at the Eastleigh Probation Office but moved to a venue at the Probation Centre in Southampton, which is a focal point for transport and is more easily accessible.

The impact of the courses

Undoubtedly one of the most attractive elements of the course for magistrates is that they can avoid lengthy delays by asking the duty probation officer to interview defendants and to explain the implications and consequences if the magistrates were to make a Probation Order with a condition that the defendant attends the course. If agreement is forthcoming magistrates can then make an immediate Order. Where complicated social circumstances or offending behaviour is detected, a full Social Enquiry Report (SER) is, of course, still requested. Magistrates were originally encouraged to make a Probation Order for six months, but it only needed a probationer to miss the beginning of one course and have a genuine reason for being unable to attend the next course for the six-month period to pass quickly. Magistrates are now requested to make an Order for twelve months, and this rarely causes problems.

Eighteen months after the course started Mrs Terri Lawrence produced an interim report based on the results of alcohol knowledge questionnaires and personal follow-up interviews with course members. However, this study now has little relevance as the present course content and structure has changed significantly. The success of the course is now measured by means of questionnaires, relating gains in alcohol knowledge, social background, criminal antecedents, and situational confidence; achievement of stated goals for attitudinal and behavioural change; and re-conviction, and will include interviews with course members at intervals of three and eighteen months after course completion. Of 109 drink-drivers who have since May 1985 completed the course, only one is recorded as having been re-convicted of a drink-drive offence. However, this figure should be regarded with caution as it does not fully account for periods of disqualification.

There was a concern that the probation officer supervising the Order, if not a course leader, may feel that his client is being dealt with in some 'specialist' way which neither demands nor requires anything further from the supervising officer. To avoid this, it is our policy to involve supervising officers as far as possible when their clients attend the course. A report to the probation officer details the course member's response and in particular all personal goals for future change in behaviour. The probation officer is required to monitor two projects which continue beyond the end of the course and has a role in providing additional support for those who wish to further reduce their alcohol consumption or indeed abstain altogether, either by direct work with the client, or by appropriate referral. Research into drink-driving is sparse and we monitor the response of course members, who all complete alcohol knowledge and situational confidence questionnaires before and after the course.

Spreading the word

In October 1985, I was invited to speak to the Annual Meeting of the Royal Society for the Prevention of Accidents (RoSPA). Two weeks prior to the meeting I was approached by the motoring correspondent of the *Daily Mail*, who was preparing cameos on each of the speakers. The course interested him and he decided to write a piece about its development and aims. The article triggered an enormous response from the media and thrust me into unaccustomed limelight and I underwent the traumatic experience of being interviewed by the press, radio, and television on something like forty occasions within two or three days. However, the publicity attracted a great deal of very positive comment and interest not only from other probation services but also road safety departments, councils on alcoholism, district health authorities, and even a large multi-national company with a fleet of drivers. The publicity was welcome because it came at a time when the Hampshire Probation Service, in association with the University of Southampton, was submitting a proposal to the Alcohol Education and Research Council (AERC) for a research grant and it may have tipped the balance in our favour. Although money for research was not forthcoming, the AERC made a counter proposal that we should design and produce a teaching pack so that others could benefit from our developmental work, thus encouraging the provision of courses in other parts of the country. In March 1986 work began on the production of the teaching pack which was completed and launched in November 1986 at a press conference in London by Mr Peter Bottomley, M.P., Minister for Roads and Traffic, and, in January 1987, at road-shows in London, Manchester, and Birmingham.

The pack contains all the materials necessary to run a course for alcohol-impaired drivers including a leaders' manual, members' handbooks, ten alcohol-level calculators, twenty-four slides, and a VHS video containing 'trigger' films for provoking discussion. The leaders' manual provides a comprehensive guide to eight two-hour sessions which go to make up the course. Packs can be obtained from: The Chief Probation Officer (Alcohol-Impaired Drivers' Course), Friary House, The Law Courts, Middle Brook Street, Winchester, SO23 8DQ. One hundred packs have now been sold in this country and abroad, and 80 per cent of the 56 probation services in England and Wales have now purchased teaching packs. Others have been bought by road safety councils, district health authorities, health education departments, councils on alcoholism, and branches of Alcohol Concern, the national alcohol body. Does your organization have a pack? Do you know of any other body which might find it useful? Does your locality provide a course for impaired drivers of the kind developed in Hampshire? Could you help to start one?

For the future, regular conferences are planned to bring together practitioners running courses and others with an interest in this field. We can all learn from each other's experiences and thus help to encourage take up, development, and refinement of the course for alcohol-impaired drivers. Why re-invent the wheel when we can all drive along together at the same speed?

Alcohol, information, and coroner's court practice

Dr Richard Whittington

The coroner has a duty to investigate any death within his or her jurisdiction which may have been caused by violence or otherwise unnaturally, and any sudden death of which the cause is unknown, and all deaths that take place whilst the individual is in custody. The coroner makes enquiries and in the majority of cases orders a post-mortem examination. As a result, since most deaths are due to natural causes, the coroner authorizes the registration of the death. In a few instances an inquest is held. An inquest is a public court of enquiry in which the findings as to who the deceased was and how, when, and where the deceased came by his death are recorded. At the conclusion of the inquest the coroner may inform any appropriate person with authority the circumstances of the death, with the purpose of preventing further fatalities. The coroner is helped in enquiry by a coroner's officer who may take statements and receive reports, documents, and other exhibits on behalf of the coroner. The coroner can authorize various tests to be done including analysis of blood and organs from the deceased person. Expert witnesses may be called. In this way the coroner gathers much useful information about the circumstances of any particular death. It is the basis of these enquiries which has enabled me as the Birmingham Coroner to take a special interest in alcohol-related deaths.

If death occurs within 12 hours of a road traffic accident, all coroners are required to ensure that analysis for blood alcohol is performed. These reports become part of the evidence and the results are relayed to the Transport and Road Research Laboratory (TRRL). In this way national statistics are compiled about the relationship between alcohol and fatal road traffic accidents. In about 28 per cent of the accidents, there is a relationship. From personal experience it is possible to obtain additional information about recent alcohol consumption which does not become available to the TRRL. For example, a 21-year-old male lost control of his car on a bend. He died three hours after the accident, but was given 30 units of blood before his death. Blood taken for cross-matching with transfused blood revealed a blood alcohol level of 134 mg per 100 ml. The second example was of a 20-year-old youth who, when drunk, fell into the path of a motor vehicle. He died 23 hours later and again blood taken in life for cross-matching purposes revealed a high alcohol content, namely 195 mg per 100 ml. Thus, a victim of a road accident may, when taken to hospital, have a massive blood transfusion before death, so that analysis would no longer be meaningful. However, it is often possible for the coroner's officer to obtain a sample of blood which has been kept in a refrigerator since shortly after admission to hospital and which was originally intended for cross-matching purposes prior to blood transfusion. Despite the fact that this sample will have no preservative analysis it can yield a useful, though approximate, blood alcohol level. A similar procedure can be followed when someone dies in hospital more than 12 hours after an accident. Increasingly doctors are becoming aware of the need to take a blood alcohol level in life. Thus if some injured person is brought to hospital and it is suspected they may be drunk, it may be helpful to determine the degree of intoxication prior to treatment. Unfortunately some young doctors are reluctant to release the results of such analysis because they mistakenly believe it is confidential information which might be defamatory to the deceased. They need instruction concerning the absurdity of this attitude since, with their colleagues, they have to cope with the disastrous consequences of drinking and driving and any information on the subject should be revealed for public examination. In addition the coroner, through enquiries, may obtain confirmation of drinking prior to any road traffic or other accident, e.g. a positive breathalyser test of the driver. From such evidence I believe that more than 30 per cent of fatal road traffic accidents are related to the misuse of alcohol.

The extent of the alcohol relationship was confirmed when a detailed analysis of 55 fatal motorcycle accidents was carried out, based on my court records, in which 24 aspects of each accident were studied, including the use of alcohol. In one-third of cases impairment of driving ability due to the taking of alcohol was apparent. Consumption of alcohol, excessive speed, and the errors of other road users were the most significant contributory factors of these fatal motorcycle accidents. Half of the victims were under 21 and the most common age at death was 17. All the drivers of the machines were male, although six female pillion passengers also died. Nearly a third of these fatalities occurred on a Friday, often in the later evening. Late-evening fatalities whatever the day of the week were particularly likely to be associated with excessive consumption of alcohol. This analysis confirmed the liability of young males to alcohol-related deaths.

As part of a more wide-ranging assessment of alcohol and unnatural death, all Birmingham inquests for the year 1980 were studied and it was found that of the 111 road traffic accidents 34 per cent were associated with misuse of alcohol. This included 38 pedestrians of whom 13 were intoxicated at the time. Drunken pedestrian deaths peaked after lunch and late-evening drinking. These findings confirmed the significant influence of alcohol on fatal road traffic accidents.

A coroner holds an inquiry into all road traffic accidents unless it is alleged that the death was due to reckless driving in which case the coroner adjourns his inquest, pending prosecution in the Crown Court, where the evidence is heard in some detail. At one time it was considered a defence to have taken alcohol, as this would have diminished the sense of responsibility so that the driver would not necessarily know what he or she was doing, or know the likely consequences of his or her action. However, attitudes are changing insofar that any person who knowingly consumes a large quantity of alcohol prior to driving a motor vehicle must appreciate the wrongness of such an act and the detrimental effect it will have on their driving with the likelihood of causing damage, injury, or death. Understandably much anger is generated following a death associated with drink and driving. Although there may be insufficient evidence, relatives often expect the driver to be tried for reckless driving. The recent consumption of alcohol prior to an accident does not on its own make the driver reckless. All the circumstances need to be known, but unfortunately the actual accident may have been incompletely witnessed so that the relevant evidence is far from complete. Indeed, not infrequently, the behaviour of the deceased may have contributed to the accident. From experience those accidents which would seem particularly likely to be related to alcohol consumption are single vehicle accidents, usually taking place in the late evening or night, in which the driver is male, young, and relatively inexperienced.

The above mentioned analysis of the 589 inquests of 1980 showed that 119 (20 per cent) were alcohol-related deaths. There were 27 alleged homicides (murder, manslaughter, infanticide, and causing death by reckless driving) of which 17 (or 63 per cent) were alcohol-related. These examples of extreme violence demonstrated that either the assailant, the victim, or both were intoxicated at the time of the incident. Twenty-one per cent of all suicides followed the recent consumption of alcohol. This can occur because drugs were taken with alcohol which enhanced their toxicity or the alcohol reduced normal caution and responsibility. Furthermore prolonged dependence on alcohol may provoke a state of intolerable isolation and despair which leads to depression which in turn causes suicide. Of the 165 deaths due to accidents in the home only 12 per cent were alcohol-related. These accidents were usually falls on the stairs or choking on vomit when drunk.

In 1980 there were 11 deaths which occurred when people were at work and of these none were alcohol-related. It is my experience as Birmingham Coroner that very few fatal accidents at work are related to the consumption of alcohol. An exception was that of a young man who fell about 70 feet from scaffolding, which he was dismantling on a Saturday afternoon following a lunchtime drinking session.

The problems for the police were highlighted as three of the persons who died whilst in police custody were affected by alcohol at the time. There is a longstanding scheme in Birmingham, sponsored by the Home Office, whereby drunks are taken to a special centre for drying-out where they can be observed by specially trained personnel rather than being incarcerated in a prison cell awaiting their appearance before the magistrates. This experiment has largely been successful with greater safety for those involved and a saving of police and court time (see 'Significant Intervention', available from Trinity Centre, Camp Hill, Birmingham 12). Overall the great majority of these alcohol-related deaths affected men, particularly those between the ages of 15 and 34, of whom 39 per cent were affected by alcohol at the time of death. Of the divorced and separated persons 44 per cent of the inquest deaths were due to alcohol-related incidents. Similarly of those of Scottish or Irish birth 45 per cent were alcohol-related deaths compared with 15 per cent for people born elsewhere. Regarding the open verdict inquest 35 per cent were alcohol-related. The evidence was confusing and intent was uncertain, so that how death occurred was unclear. However, many of these deaths were probably avoidable.

In 1980 all deaths that were apparently due to alcohol, even if this was a chronic abuse, were reported to the coroner. These deaths from diseases such as liver cirrhosis, cardiomyopathy, and dementia were dealt with without an inquest. Twelve per cent of this group were Sikhs, though it was estimated that only 4 per cent of the Birmingham population were of this ethnic group. Sikhs therefore appear vulnerable to the effects of excessive drinking. The mere consumption of a large quantity of alcohol may alone be the cause of a sudden death. During 1980 11 people died from the effects of acute alcoholism, which is a medical emergency and demands urgent comprehensive treatment in hospital.

The consumption of alcohol with drugs is particularly dangerous as the presence of alcohol enhances the toxicity of the drugs. In recent years dextropropoxyphene usually combined with paracetamol has been an increasingly popular pain-relieving drug. It gained the reputation for safety, effectiveness, and freedom from side effects. By 1979 there were an increasing number of deaths caused by this drug usually prescribed in the form of distalgesic. These deaths were commonly of young persons and often followed the consumption of alcohol. Many of the deaths were thought not necessarily suicidal, being merely the result of impulsive overdosing often under the influence of alcohol. Unfortunately the deaths took place very rapidly before treatment could take place and usually outside hospital. Consequently it was only coroners and forensic scientists who knew of the danger and doctors were continuing to prescribe the drug. A series of scientific papers, including some from the Birmingham Coroner's Office, beginning in 1979, drew attention to the danger of this drug, and as a result many changes have occurred in the prescribing patterns of this drug. Undoubtedly the public interest in the writing and speaking of a coroner helped to promote suspicion of the dangers of dextropropoxyphene. Journals as different as the *Guardian* newspaper (16 March 1983) and *Private Eye* (28 February 1982) took up the cause. As a consequence distalgesic is no longer prescribable under the National Health

Service and a comparable drug, though available, is prescribed in much smaller quantities. Every bottle and packet has a warning that alcohol should not be taken with the tablets.

Distalgesic is an extreme example of the danger of taking drugs with alcohol. Of particular danger are the sedatives, tranquillizers, and anti-depressants which are frequently in the hands of those who are emotionally disturbed and temperamentally irresponsible. Thus a small overdose on its own may not be fatal but in combination with alcohol may cause death. On some occasions such overdoses are clearly not intended to be self-destructive but an accidental fatal overdose has just as grave consequences.

There have been recent changes in the coroners' law (Coroners' Rules, 1984) such that a coroner now seldom sits with a jury in his court, he or she no longer has to personally view each body, and it is no longer permitted for a coroner to commit someone to trial in the High Court on a charge of murder. Until recently doctors and registrars were obliged to notify the coroner of any death that was alcohol-related. This included those deaths that were attributed to chronic misuse of alcohol. It has been said that doctors refrained from mentioning alcohol on the death certificate in an attempt to protect relatives from the disgrace of an alcohol-related death and having it reported to the coroner, though few coroners would actually hold an inquest. It is to be hoped that doctors will now be more honest and accurate when completing their death certificates in relation to longstanding alcohol problems. Naturally, deaths from acute alcoholic poisoning are still reportable. Recently the Home Office has introduced a new recommended verdict (Coroners' Rules, 1984). This is of death by 'non-dependent abuse of drugs'. As indicated, many drug-related deaths were not suicidal and they may well have been unintentional accidents. However, there is always a doubt, especially if alcohol was consumed, concerning the intention. Many such inquests ended with an open verdict as the evidence was insufficient to come to a conclusion. It is hoped the use of the verdict, 'death by non-dependent abuse of drugs', will reduce the number of open verdicts. A variation is sometimes used in Birmingham, namely, the verdict of 'death by non-dependent abuse of drugs and alcohol', as this more adequately reflects the circumstances.

My interest in transport and safety led to an invitation to be one of the Trustees of the Parliamentary Advisory Council on Transport and Safety (PACTS). This is an organization with members in both Houses of Parliament which promotes research and in particular helps to prepare Bills on transport safety. For instance, the seat-belt legislation was largely guided through Parliament with the help of PACTS. PACTS is campaigning to introduce random breath testing of drivers by the police, based on overseas' experience. PACTS would also like to reduce the maximum permissible blood alcohol level from 80 mg per 100 ml to 50 mg per 100 ml. Since young and inexperienced drivers are particularly susceptible to the effects of alcohol it is suggested that 20 mg of alcohol per 100 ml of blood should be the maximum permitted for this group. I was able to submit these ideas recently to the Transport Minister in a personal interview. He was particularly interested in the idea that insurance companies should warn clients of the inflated costs of reinsuring after a drink-related driving licence suspension.

Over the past few years I have accepted numerous invitations to speak on various aspects of alcohol misuse, sometimes to doctors but also to a variety of other groups. There was recently created in Birmingham a group concerned with promoting interest in limiting drinking and driving. Unfortunately, a recent conference for driving instructors, aimed to obtain their involvement, was cancelled through lack of support. Success is hoped for in other fields of persuasion and publicity. Effective publicity is important if the message is to reach and convince the public to a degree that people will refuse to be driven by any person who is thought to have been drinking. A coroner's remarks may attract media attention, as did my speech to the meeting of the British Medical Association in Newcastle-upon-Tyne in 1980. I pointed out that alcohol had become relatively cheap compared to the rise in personal incomes in recent years. The local paper headlined their report with 'The Pound a Pint Coroner'. This was just the impact that was intended. Alcohol is too cheap, since the price has not advanced with the cost of living, so permitting consumption to increase dangerously. Though education has a part in moulding the public's attitude to the danger of excessive consumption and misuse of alcohol, the most effective way of curbing excessive consumption and abuse is by substantially increasing the price as has been done in the past. Clearly this is where the Chancellor of the Exchequer can influentially play a part in improving the health and safety of the nation. Unfortunately, successive Budgets have been devised without tackling this issue so that now a dramatic rise would have to be introduced to restore relative values and this might be politically unacceptable, unless it were done in stages.

Starting CADD: campaign against drinking and driving

John Knight

So you have an issue that you feel needs addressing, or perhaps there is an aspect of life that you feel is harmful and could be improved, or is downright wrong and something should be done about it. What can you do? A first reaction would be to seek out an already existing group and join it. You could then add your energies to those already in the field of action which you think is worthwhile. But suppose you look around and find nobody is working in the area of your particular concern, or what is being done does not seem to be the best approach, or even relevant to the problem as you see it. You would have to go it alone or persuade others to join you and start a new initiative. This brings you to a first decision. If you decide to go it alone you will be free to say and do just what appeals to you, just what you want, but you will be a lone voice. In these days of the mass media of television, press, and radio, you will find it difficult to be heard above all their noise. If you want to be more effective, to make a greater impact more quickly, you must find a few people who share your concern and are prepared to devote some of their time and energy to the problem. When just one other person joins you your human resources are doubled. Four more will quadruple them.

It might be difficult to find these first supporters for your campaign, especially if you do not see any obvious help from among your own friends and acquaintances. You must then look further afield by making enquiries among those working in allied fields, or by writing to your local press, or seeking help from your local radio. When you have gathered a small group you must then arrange to meet. You will need to plan this meeting carefully. There will be two different parts to your time together: getting to know each other and the business of the meeting. Faced with a group of comparative strangers it can be difficult to keep a first meeting concentrated on the subject. You should try to create a situation where ideas will flow. You will need to have some ideas of your own and some questions that will stimulate discussion and reactions. You should make sure that everyone in the group gets ample opportunity to take part even if this means that you have to ask direct questions of anyone who seems to be shy or has difficulty in pushing themselves forward.

An agenda or short list of topics that can be circulated before you meet will allow some preparation by everyone who is attending. Try to have somebody who will take notes of the important issues raised and any conclusions that may be reached, or definite decisions made. You may need a number of meetings before you formulate a definite policy with specific aims and it is well worth spending some time on this.

Sooner or later you will need to consider just how you are going to disseminate your ideas to a wider public. Here you can consider a direct approach to existing local societies and organizations who would welcome a speaker at some of their meetings. You will need someone from your group who is prepared to take on such public speaking engagements. A source of information about local organizations would be very helpful. In many areas the local paper may publish a 'Citizen's Guide'. This can be a veritable mine of information on local organizations. There will be many more than you think. Another way to get your message across is to use the local media, particularly the local press and radio. It is useful to keep in mind that they face each day with a blank sheet or silent minutes to fill. This means they are always looking for items of news or interest. The other side of this is that they will always try to have much more material than they can use.

An engagement to talk to a local group will concentrate the mind and should really compel you to think out your ideas and how to put them over. Even if you make a hash of it the first time you will learn something from the experience and be in a better position next time. Nobody gets it right first time. It is always a good thing to have two speakers, each undertaking to talk about a different aspect of your subject. This makes it easier for each person and helps the audience to keep their attention from wandering too far. To make a talk more interesting it is a good idea to have some kind of display material on show. The preparation of this might well be a means of using other people in your group. They would, of course, want to set it up and attend the meeting.

Illustrate your points by quoting actual, personal experience of local people with their permission. No need to give names. Always allow plenty of time for discussion and questions. Audience participation makes the event much more worthwhile. This can be difficult to start as you will often find nobody wants to be the first one to speak. If you have someone from your group present in the audience they will probably get the ball rolling with the first contribution.

Having made a start in this way you will be in a better position to write to your local paper. This could be in the form of a letter or an article, and it will be more likely to be printed if you can time it to exploit a topical news item which has only recently been in the paper.

Interviews on the local radio or television require some careful preparation. Time is always short and in the first stages one can easily be overawed by the occasion and find oneself lost for words. The best approach is to prepare for your interview and to decide to make just two or three points. You may find it helpful to write trigger words on to the palm of your hand. In this way you can look down at your palm without anyone knowing just what you are up to. If the interviewer starts to ask questions you have not prepared for, it is a good idea to make a short reply and then say, 'But have you considered this point?'; then you can get back to the points you have prepared. Here again it is very helpful to have someone else with you who can come in if you pause at a loss for words. In these situations a game is being played out. The interviewer will be more experienced than you are and will want the session to be as spontaneous as possible. He will probably have a good idea of the area of his questions and may help you by telling you this, but he may not tell you the exact questions he has prepared. He will often put in a quite unexpected question at the end and a brief pause for you to think before answering will add to the spontaneity.

Interviews on television have a risk for which you need to be prepared. The interviewer will want to put you at ease and establish a relaxed atmosphere but do not allow this to distract you from the seriousness of your subject. If you watch members of the public being interviewed on television you will often see a smile flit across their face even when their subject is tragic. This may result from a too relaxed and lighthearted preparation for your interview or from a feeling you may have which is pleasing because you are elated that someone is at last taking an interest in your work.

If you are successful in your venture a time will come when you will need to think of your legal status. At first you will be a group of individuals each of whom will be responsible for his or her own actions and behaviour. This will not be satisfactory if you are to grow into an effective organization. You will need a legal entity to lift responsibility from individuals to the group. This will basically open up two possibilities: charitable status or the formation of a company limited by guarantee. There are some very important advantages in becoming a charity and these include freedom from liability for VAT and, in some cases, from local rates. Perhaps the biggest advantage is to be found in the link between charities. The key for you rests in the fact that charities can only use their funds for the purpose clearly stated in their deeds, and a charity can only give funds to another charity. This means that if you become one you would be eligible to receive help from others in similar fields. You would not be able to receive financial help from a charity if you were not yourself a charity and a valuable source of help would be denied you. However, there are a few trusts that can help to promote worthwhile causes and they usually see their role as providing 'seed money'. It can be a lengthy business getting this kind of help as there is always a long waiting list and you have to put up a very good case. Charitable work is grouped under three headings: relief of poverty, religion, and education. Your needs would most likely come under the last category. When the time comes to consider charitable status you can get some help from the National Council of Voluntary Organizations at 26 Bedford Square, London, WC13 3HU (01-636 4066). They will give you an hour's interview and discussion without charge so you will need to have a clear idea of your aims and needs before you make an appointment. After the first hour there is a charge of £20.00. Such an interview is only the beginning. It can take a very long time to the final achievement of actual charitable status. You will need to think in terms of at least one year or longer. Your next move would be a formal application to the Charity Commissioners at 60 Haymarket, London, SW1. There are 158,000 charities with a total annual disposable income of £10 billion.

If you cannot wait or there is a serious difficulty you can get a legal status or entity by forming a company limited by guarantee and with no share capital. This is a much easier option. The only benefit it confers is that the directors' liability is limited to a fixed sum which can be as little as £1. The main drawback to this is that you would find it difficult to borrow money because of the limited guarantee. This need not be a disadvantage if you can organize your own fund-raising either by membership or by other activities. The easiest way to achieve this is to put it in the hands of a solicitor, but it will cost money. An alternative would be to get one of your group to look it up in the library or go direct to someone who sells 'off the shelf companies'. One such is Jordan & Sons Ltd., London (01-253 3030) or one of their local branches. The solicitors' Law Stationery Society or Oyez might be helpful at 27 Crimscott Street, London, SE1 5TS.

As your numbers grow you will need to keep records, especially if you become a legal entity. The use of a home computer will help here. You will need a secretary, treasurer, and a chairperson. These people will inevitably become the spokespeople for your group and it is a good idea to be clear just who has authority to speak for you, especially to the media, who will want immediate response if you are to make the most use of their help. You should have someone who is always available by phone and be sure to give the name and phone number on all communications. There will often be occasions when you will be misquoted and a quick response will be required to correct this.

When your numbers grow you will need a means of keeping everyone in touch with all that is going on. Key people will give more time to your work and will be more willing to attend meetings. Inevitably there will be others who are only on the fringe and who will give less time but are nevertheless important to your work and will need to be kept in touch with all that is going on. Most organizations have a pyramidal structure with a wide base of members whose contribution is small but important because of their numbers. Some kind of newsletter or magazine will require an editor and provide scope for another key person. Perhaps there is a member with a word processor. Modern technology makes this very much easier.

When you have reached this stage you are well on your way and you need only to keep up the momentum. Good luck.

Drinking and driving: raising the issue

Mike McKnight

Between 1984 and 1987 in Birmingham, there were approximately 1,000 casualties in drink-drive accidents with twenty deaths and over 900 injuries. In monetary terms this equates to approximately £1.5 million per annum, although drink-related accidents raise this figure to approximately £6 million. Accident analysis also shows that the problem does not solely relate to the Christmas period but that it is an all-the-year-round problem, with peaks at Christmas and midsummer.

Armed with this information, a seminar was jointly organized by Birmingham City Council and Aquarius, in November 1986. It became apparent at the seminar that more could and should be done if a reduction in drink-drive accidents was to be achieved. The City Engineers Road Safety Unit drew together various organizations and invited representatives to form a working group to take a serious look at the problem. The group is organized and run by Birmingham City Council with Dr Richard Whittington, HM coroner for Birmingham and Solihull, chairing the group. Contributions to the group include: Aquarius, the police, the health education department, driving schools associations, probation and aftercare, licensed victuallers, the Brewers Society, local radio, and RoSPA.

The aims of the group are simple and basic:

- to make people more aware of the dangers of drinking and driving;
- to bring about a behavioural and attitudinal change in the driving public; and
- to reduce drink-drive-related accidents.

One of the first projects organized by Aquarius was a series of evening lectures entitled 'What shall we do with the drunken driver?' Speakers included HM Coroner, a road safety officer, and members of RoSPA, the police, and the Brewers Society.

Birmingham City Council has responded in a positive way and the Chairman of the Technical Services and Road Safety Sub-Committee, Councillor Matt Redmond, has authorized the use of local authority vehicles to carry drink-driving messages. For a city the size of Birmingham, this represents a huge area of 'advertising' space. The idea has drawn considerable interest from other departments in the city, such as health education, social services, and police support vehicles. The West Midlands Ambulance Service have shown an interest and have proceeded with carrying the message 'We see the misery – Don't Drink and Drive' on most of their ambulance fleet.

The Birmingham Superprix attracts many thousands of spectators and as part of the drink-drive programme the chosen theme was along the same lines. A national company marketing low-alcohol lager was contacted and they agreed to provide their products free of charge to the public. The idea was to persuade the driving public to drink alternative drinks which would not impair their driving nor place them in an illegal position, thus ensuring a safer journey home from the event. The idea proved to be very successful and over the two-day period thousands of cans of the drink were distributed. In addition the Road Safety Unit ran a competition with a radio cassette recorder, watches, sweatshirts, etc., as prizes.

To support the Department of Transport's drink-drive campaign the group decided to use the local press to convey the message of 'Drink or Drive – Not Both'. 400,000 copies of a four-page pull-out supplement were distributed through a local newspaper. The contents of the supplement gave useful advice on when holding a party to ensure driving guests stayed safe and legally under the limit. It also advised on how to enjoy someone else's party, what drinks were available, and where to get those drinks.

The Birmingham drink-drive group meet regularly to suggest new ways to project the message that drinking and driving wrecks lives. The group intend to carry their aims and objectives throughout the year until such time as drink-drive accidents are reduced considerably. That time is getting closer.

Index